AN APPLE A DAY COOKBOOK

AN APPLE A DAY COOKBOOK

Susan Smith

THIRD EYE
LONDON · CANADA
2000

An Apple a Day Cookbook

Canadian Cataloguing in Publication Data

Smith, Susan, 1951
An apple a day cookbook

ISBN 0-919581-66-8

1. Cookery (Apples). I. Title.
2. TX813.A6S64 2000 641.6'411 C00-931848-8

Cover Drawing by
Astara Ali

Published by
Third Eye Publications
31 Clarke Road
London, Ont., Canada
N5W 5W5

FROM THE AUTHOR.....

Thank you for your interest in *An Apple A Day Cookbook*. Sales from the *1st Edition* resulted in many questions and suggestions.

I feel that this *2nd Edition* incorporates those suggestions and answers the questions for you. You will find exactly the same recipes in this edition as in the first; the directions may be improved upon but they are essentially the same.

I have been delighted with the response to the book and thank everyone who has contributed their recipes, ideas, time and effort to make it the success it is.

Susan Smith
Author

An Apple a day keeps the doctor AWEIGH !

AN APPLE A DAY
KEEPS THE DOCTOR AWEIGH!

That's right! Eaten instead of junk food, apples offer a quick, nutritious, LoCal way to keep both your weight and your waist down!

And not since the legendary days of Johnny Appleseed have so many bushels of apples been sown across this fertile land.

In this cookbook, Susan Smith has gotten to the core of the apple lover's day, starting with breakfast suggestions like barbecue-baked apple ... double decker apple dessert for dinner and various apple salads and sauces for supper!

These and many more - along with tips for canning, freezing, storing and squeezing. So don't let this doctor keep you away from these tempting apple treats.

Enjoy!

A.B. CHERNICK, M.D., FRCS (C), FACOG

INDEX - OVERVIEW

INDEX

SECTION A - BAKED APPLES

SECTION B - APPLESAUCE

SECTION C - APPLES WITH MEAT, WITH VEGETABLES AND AS SNACKS

SECTION C - APPLES WITH MEAT, WITH VEGETABLES AND AS SNACKS - Continued

SECTION D - PUDDINGS, COBBLERS, & OTHER DESSERTS

SECTION E - JAMS, JELLIES, GLAZES

SECTION F - BEVERAGES

SECTION G - CANDIES, COOKIES, SQUARES

SECTION H - CANNING

SECTION I - FREEZING

SECTION J - CRAFTS

SECTION K - PIES, CRISPS AND CRUMBLES

SECTION K - PIES, CRISPS AND CRUMBLES - Continued

SECTION L - CAKES

SECTION L - CAKES - Continued

SECTION M - MUFFINS

SECTION N - CREPES AND PANCAKES

SECTION 0 - SALADS

SECTION 0 - SALADS - Continued

SECTION P - TIPS AND HELPFUL INFORMATION

SECTION A

BAKED APPLES

BAKED APPLES

Choose baking apples such as Rome Beauty, Starr, Jersey Red, Winesap, Northern Spy, Golden Delicious or Greening. Select one apple per person.

Heat oven to 375°F. Core apples; remove 1-inch strip of skin around middle of each apple or peel upper half of each to prevent skin from splitting.

Place apples upright in baking dish. Fill centre of each apple with 1 to 2 tbsp granulated white or brown sugar, 1 tsp butter or margarine and 1/8 tsp cinnamon. Pour water (1/4" deep) into baking dish.

Bake about 30 to 40 minutes or until apples are tender when pierced with fork. (Time will vary with size and variety of apple.) If desired, spoon syrup in pan over apples several times during baking.

VARIATION: Red Cinnamon Baked Apples:

Omit butter and cinnamon and place 1 tablespoon plus 2 tsp red cinnamon candies in centre of each apple. Spoon syrup in pan over apples several times during baking.

VARIATION: Maple Syrup Baked Apples:

Fill the core cavity with equal quantities of butter and maple syrup to which a few raisins and a dash of cinnamon have been added. Bake for approx. 30 minutes at 350°F. Serve hot.

BAKED APPLE - MICROWAVE VARIATION

1 cooking apple (per person)
1 1/2 tbsp brown sugar
2 tsp butter or margarine
cinnamon

Core and peel a rim from the top of the apple to let the steam escape. Combine brown sugar and butter. Fill cavity. Sprinkle cinnamon over top and peeled portion. Cook 2 minutes, or until apple is almost tender. Let apple stand 5 minutes to complete the cooking.

When cooking several apples at a time, add 1 additional minute per apple.

BAKED APPLE - BARBECUE VARIATION

corn syrup
large green apples
brown sugar
cinnamon
nutmeg
raisins
butter or margarine

Core the apples and peel a third of the way down from the stem end. Fill the centres with a mixture of brown sugar, cinnamon, nutmeg and raisins. Brush the peeled surface with corn syrup and put about 1/2 tsp of butter or margarine on each. Wrap securely in aluminum foil.

Barbecue for 1 hour on the grill until the apples are tender.

APPLES BAKED IN RED WINE

4 firm baking apples
1 cup brown sugar
pinch nutmeg
2 whole cloves
small piece of cinnamon stick
2 cups red wine
1 cup water

Preheat oven to 375°F.

Core apples, but do not pierce them completely through bottoms. Peel tops a little less than half way down, leaving remaining skin intact.

Put apples, peeled halves up, in a deep baking dish of a size to hold them closely together. Fill centres of the apples with some of the sugar.

Add whole cloves, cinnamon stick, wine and water to dish. Add remaining sugar, coating tops of apples generously and putting rest into wine.

Bake 30-40 minutes, until apples are tender.

CRUNCHY BAKED APPLES WITH BRAN FLAKES

1 cup bran flakes
1/2 cup all-purpose flour
1/2 cup firmly packed brown sugar
1/2 tsp cinnamon
1/4 cup butter
6 medium apples

Combine bran flakes, flour, sugar and cinnamon. Cut in butter until mixture is crumbly.

Preheat oven to 375°F.

Peel and core apples. Run tines of fork around apples to make deep indentations. Pat crumb mixture evenly over surface of apples to coat completely. Place on shallow metal baking pan. Bake 20-25 minutes, or until fork-tender. Serve warm, topped with whipped cream, if desired.

Makes 6 servings.

GRANOLA BAKED APPLES

4 cooking apples (cored)
3/4 cup granola cereal
2 tbsp brown sugar
sour cream (optional)

Cut out centre of apples to leave a 1/2" shell. Chop 1/2 cup apple from the centre and set aside. Cut a strip of peel 1/2" wide around top of apple. In medium bowl mix the apple which has been set aside with the granola and brown sugar. Fill scooped out apples.

Place in shallow baking dish; add 1/4" water to bottom. Cover and bake in 350°F oven 45 minutes, or until apples are tender. Serve with sour cream, if desired.

Serves 4.

BAKED APPLES STUFFED WITH SAUSAGE

7 tart apples, weighing about 1/4 lb each
2 tbsp lemon juice
1 1/4 cups hot beef broth
salt, to taste

STUFFING:

1/4 cup margarine or butter
1 onion, grated
1/2 lb pork sausage meat
1/2 cup soft white bread crumbs
1 tsp dried sage
finely grated rind of 1 lemon
pinch of ground nutmeg
pepper, to taste

Preheat oven to 400°F.

To make the stuffing, melt half the margarine in a saucepan, add the onion and cook gently for 5 minutes. Tip the cooked onion into a bowl.

Melt the remaining margarine in the saucepan, add the sausage meat and cook over moderate heat, stirring with a wooden spoon to remove any lumps, until the sausage meat is evenly browned. Using a slotted spoon, remove the sausage meat and add to the onion. Stir in the bread crumbs, sage and lemon rind and season to taste with nutmeg and pepper.

Using a sharp knife, core each apple to within 1/2 inch of the base. Then widen each hole to 1 1/2 inches. Make lengthwise cuts in the skin of the apple around each hole to prevent apples from bursting while they are cooking.

Using a spoon, fill the apples with the stuffing, pressing it down well into each cavity. Arrange the apples in a heat-proof dish. Mix the lemon juice into the hot broth, and season to taste, then pour it around the apples.

Bake uncovered, for about 35 minutes, until the apples are tender. Transfer the apples to a warmed serving dish and serve at once with the broth served separately in warmed pitcher.

Serves 4.

HONEY POACHED APPLES

1 tbsp cornstarch
1 tsp ginger
1/3 cup liquid honey
1/2 cup water
2 tbsp brandy (optional)
1 tbsp lemon juice
6 medium apples
2 tbsp butter or margarine

Combine first 6 ingredients in small bowl. Peel and core apples; cut into lengthwise halves.

Melt butter in large frying pan over medium heat. Stir in honey mixture. Cook and stir until mixture comes to a boil. Place apples, cut side down, in pan. Cover and simmer for 8 to 10 minutes, or until fork-tender, turning apples once during cooking. Serve warm with ice cream, if desired.

Makes 6 servings.

HONEY BAKED APPLES WITH WALNUTS

4 large apples cored
3 tbsp honey
1/2 cup chopped walnuts
2 tbsp butter or margarine
1/2 cup raisins
1 1/2 cups water
1 tsp cornstarch
2 tsp cold water
juice of 1/2 lemon
juice of 1/2 orange

Preheat oven to 375°F.

Peel only upper half of apples. Coat peeled part with honey and roll in walnuts. Place apples in roasting pan.

Divide butter and raisins into 4 parts and insert in cavities in apples. Squeeze fruit juices over apples and sprinkle with cinnamon. Pour 1 1/2 cups water into roasting pan and bake 40 minutes or until tender. Cooking time may need to be adjusted, depending on variety of apple.

When cooked, transfer apples to serving platter. Place roasting pan with juices over high heat and bring to boil.

Mix cornstarch with 2 tbsp cold water; stir into sauce until well mixed. Reduce heat and continue cooking 1 minute or until sauce is thickened.

Pour sauce over apples and chill. Serve cold.

Makes 4 servings (approximately 321 calories each).

APPLE DUMPLINGS - VARIATION 1

(A baked apple wrapped in tender, golden pastry)

Pastry for 9-inch two-crust pie
(See PIE Section pages 108 & 109)
6 baking apples, peeled and cored
(each apple about 3 inches in diameter)
3 tbsp raisins
3 tbsp chopped nuts
2 cups brown sugar (packed)
1 cup water

Heat oven to 425°F. Prepare pastry; roll 2/3 of dough into 14" square; cut into 4 squares. Roll remaining dough into rectangle 14"x 7", cut into 2 squares. Place 1 apple on each square.

Mix raisins and nuts; fill centre of each apple. Moisten corners of squares; bring 2 opposite corners of pastry up over apple and press together. Fold in sides of remaining corners (as if wrapping a package); bring corners up over apple and press together. Place dumplings in ungreased baking dish, 11 1/2"x 7 1/2"x 1 1/2".

Heat brown sugar and water to boiling; carefully pour around dumplings. Spooning syrup over dumplings 2 or 3 times during baking, bake about 40 minutes or until crust is golden and apples are tender. Serve warm or cool; if desired, top with sweetened whipping cream. Makes 6 servings.

VARIATION:

Peach Dumplings:

Substitute 6 fresh peaches, peeled and halved, for the apples and 1/4 cup cranberry relish for the raisins and nuts.

APPLE DUMPLINGS - VARIATION 2

Pastry for pie crust (see PIE Section pg. 108 & 109)
6 medium apples (peeled and cored)
6 tsp red currant jelly

SPICE MIXTURE:

3 tbsp butter or margarine
3/4 tsp cinnamon
3/4 tsp allspice
3/4 tsp nutmeg
1/4 tsp cloves
1/3 cup brown sugar (lightly packed)

TO PREPARE:

Preheat oven to 375°F. Lightly grease a large shallow baking dish.

Roll out pastry to 1/8" thick to form a rectangle 18" x 12". Cut into 6 squares. Place one apple on each square of pastry and add 1 tsp red currant jelly to each. Spread Spice Mixture over each apple; bring the points of each square together and seal. Place in prepared baking dish. Bake for 30 minutes.

SAUCE:

1 1/2 cups boiling water
1 1/2 cups granulated sugar
3 tbsp apple juice or water

Combine ingredients for sauce in small pan; cook until sugar is dissolved. Pour over baked apples and bake for an additional 20 minutes, basting frequently. Serve warm.

SECTION B

APPLESAUCE

APPLESAUCE

4 medium cooking apples, peeled, quartered & cored
1 cup water
1/2 cup brown sugar (packed)
1/4 tsp cinnamon
1/8 tsp nutmeg

Heat apples and water over medium heat to boiling. Reduce heat and simmer, stirring occasionally, 5 to 10 minutes or until tender. Stir in brown sugar, cinnamon and nutmeg; heat to boiling.

Makes about 4 cups.

MICROWAVE APPLESAUCE

4 medium cooking apples, peeled, quartered & cored
1/2 cup water
3/4 cup brown sugar (packed)
1/2 tsp cinnamon

Place apples and water in a 1 1/2 quart microwavable casserole dish. Cover and cook 10 minutes or until apples are tender, stirring after 5 minutes. Mash apples with fork. Stir in sugar and cinnamon. Cool.

Serves 6.

NOTE: Refer to Section I (page 95) for information on Freezing Applesauce

FRESH BLENDER APPLESAUCE

4 large apples, peeled, cored, quartered
1/2 cup water
3 tsp honey
1/8 to 1/4 tsp ground cinnamon

Place all ingredients in container of electric blender. Blend at medium speed until smooth, about 1 minute. Serve at room temperature or chill. Makes 3 cups, or six 1/2 cup servings.

NO FUSS STOVE-TOP APPLESAUCE

1/2 cup water
1/4 to 1/2 cup sugar
juice of 1/2 a lemon
2 unpeeled apples, grated

Squeeze the juice of 1/2 a lemon. Add to it the grated apples. Stir well.

Bring water and sugar to a fast, rolling boil. Pour apples into the boiling hot syrup. Stir until well mixed. Remove from heat. Pour into a dish. Cover and let stand until cool.

Refrigerate.

POTATOES STUFFED WITH APPLESAUCE

4 large baking potatoes, cooked in skins*
1 cup applesauce
1 cup sour cream
3 tbsp bacon bits or crumbled cooked bacon
2 tbsp chives or green onion, chopped
1/2 cup butter or margarine
1/2 tsp salt

* TO BAKE POTATOES:

Wash potatoes and remove any "eyes"; wrap in foil. Bake in 400°F oven for approximately 1 hour.

OR

Bake in Microwave Oven - wash potatoes; place a small towel on the bottom of your microwave oven; space potatoes evenly on towel. Cover with towel; bake on high approximately 15 minutes.

STUFFING:

Cut cooked and slightly cooled potatoes lengthwise. Scoop out centres, leaving skins intact. Mash cooked potato centres and blend with remaining ingredients. Fill potato shells with mixture and place in a 9" x 13" glass baking dish. Bake in conventional oven at 375°F for approximately 30 minutes or in Microwave oven on Medium for approximately 15 minutes.

Serves 6 to 8.

SECTION C

WITH MEAT
WITH VEGETABLES
AND AS SNACKS

APPLE SOUP

12 large apples
2 tbsp sugar
1/2 lb raisins (boiled until soft)
1 tbsp potato (uncooked & pureed)

Quarter 12 large apples. Put them in a pan with boiling water. When the soup has a strong taste of apples, strain it through nylon mesh* and add more water until there are about nine pints. Add 2 tbsp. sugar, 1/2 lb. raisins, first boiled until soft. Thicken with 1 tbsp. potato puree. Serve well chilled.

* Old panty hose (washed and bleached) serve very well to strain foods.

APPLE CURRY SOUP

2 cans condensed beef consomme
2 cans water
1 large apple, grated
1 small onion, chopped
1 cup cream
salt and pepper, to taste
curry powder, to taste

Cook the consomme, apple and onion together until tender, about 5-10 minutes. Strain to remove apples and onions or puree in electric blender.

Stir in the cream and season to taste with salt, pepper and curry.

Reheat soup but do not boil. Garnish with a little grated apple.

Serves 4.

APPLE FRITTERS

4 medium-sized apples, cored, peeled
3 tbsp sugar
3 tsp lemon juice
4 tbsp brandy

Cut apples in eight pieces (two cuts top to bottom and one cross-wise). Place pieces in shallow dish. Sprinkle with sugar, lemon juice and brandy. Marinate 2 hours and drain.

Fritter Batter:

3/4 cup all-purpose flour
1/2 cup milk
1/4 cup heavy cream
2 eggs, well beaten
pinch of salt
pinch of pepper
1 tsp baking powder
1 tsp olive oil

In a mixing bowl, blend flour into milk. Add cream, eggs, salt, pepper, baking powder and olive oil. Mix well.

Dip drained apples in batter.

Heat at least 1 inch of olive oil in skillet. Fry dipped apples until golden. Sprinkle with icing sugar at once and serve warm.

VARIATION: use 4 ripe bananas - prepare the same way as apples.

Makes 4 servings.

APPLE AND CHEESE TOASTS

(Tasty snack takes only 10-15 minutes to prepare and cook)

5 small eating apples
1/4 cup margarine or butter
1/4 cup shredded Old Cheddar
  OR crumbled Danish blue cheese
1/4 cup cottage cheese
4 slices bread

Quarter, core and peel 4 apples. Melt the margarine in a skillet. Add apple slices and cook over moderate heat for about 3 minutes until they are golden and puffy. Using a spatula, gently transfer to a plate.

Preheat the broiler to high.

Place the Cheddar (or Danish Blue) cheese into a bowl. Add the cottage cheese and mix thoroughly with a fork to blend.

Toast the bread on 1 side only. Place the cooked apple slices on the untoasted sides of the bread, then top with the cheese mixture.

Return to the broiler and toast for 4-5 minutes, until the cheese is bubbling and golden. Slice the remaining apple and place on top of the toasts to garnish. Serve at once.

NOTE: To reduce calories, you may use only cottage cheese.

For a filling meal, double the quantities and serve with salad.

APPLE AND AVOCADO BROIL

2 ripe avocados
4 crisp eating apples
2 tbsp margarine
1/4 cup all-purpose flour
1 1/4 cups milk
1/2 cup shredded Cheddar Cheese
2 tsp Dijon mustard
salt and pepper, to taste
juice of 1/2 lemon
1/2 cup soft, whole wheat bread crumbs

Preheat the broiler to high. Because Avocados quickly turn black if exposed to air they should be prepared just before they are needed.

To make the sauce, melt the margarine in a small saucepan, sprinkle in the flour and stir over a low heat for 1-2 minutes, until it is straw-coloured. Remove from the heat and gradually stir in the milk. Return to the heat and simmer, stirring until thick and smooth. Stir in 1/2 cup of the cheese and the mustard. Add salt and pepper to taste. Stir until the cheese has melted; remove from heat.

Peel the avocados, cut in half and remove the seeds. Cut lengthwise into thin slices. Peel, quarter and core the apples. Cut into thin slices. Arrange the slices of avocado and apple in layers in 4 individual au gratin dishes. Squeeze the lemon juice over them to prevent discoloration.

Pour the sauce over the avocado and apple. Mix together the remaining cheese and the bread crumbs. Sprinkle evenly over the top. Broil 5 minutes and serve. Makes 4 servings.

SPICED APPLE RINGS

These spicy rings are especially festive at Christmas time.

6 cups granulated white sugar
1 1/2 cups cider vinegar
1 tsp red food colouring (optional)
4 whole cinnamon sticks
2 tsp whole cloves
4 lbs firm, ripe Golden Delicious apples
(peeled and cored)

Place sugar in a 5-quart pot along with vinegar, food colouring (if used), cinnamon, and cloves. Bring mixture to a boil, uncovered; reduce heat and simmer for 10 minutes.

Slice apples crosswise into rings 1/3" thick. Add the rings to the simmering syrup and cook, turning rings occasionally, for 6 to 8 minutes or until apples are barely tender and just becoming translucent around the edges.

Place fruit in **sterilized** canning jars and fill to 1/2" from rim with hot liquid. Carefully wipe rim and place lid on each jar as it is filled. Screw on ring band as tightly as you comfortably can; set jars on a folded towel away from drafts to cool. Test seal by pressing lid with your finger. If it stays down when pressed, jar is sealed and may be stored in a cool, dry place indefinitely. If lid pops back up; seal is not airtight and fruit should be stored in refrigerator until eaten.

Store at least 1 week before using. Refrigerate after opening.

TOMATO-APPLE RELISH

4 lbs firm ripe tomatoes
3 large apples
4 cups finely chopped onion
2 green bell peppers, (seeds removed and finely chopped)
2 red bell peppers, (seeds removed and finely chopped)
1 cup raisins
1 cup cider vinegar
3/4 cup firmly packed brown sugar
1 tbsp mustard seed
1 tbsp salt
1 tbsp turmeric
1 1/2 tsp celery seed

Peel tomatoes and chop coarsely; you should have 6 cups. Peel apples and chop coarsely (4 cups).

Place all ingredients in a 4-5 quart pot. Bring to a boil over high heat, stirring occasionally. Reduce heat to medium-low and continue to cook, uncovered until mixture is quite thick and liquid has been absorbed (about 1 hour).

Pour hot mixture in 4 sterilized pint-sized canning jars. Fill to 1/2 inch from rim. Carefully wipe rim dry and place lid on each jar as it is filled. Screw on ring band as tightly as you comfortably can; set jars on a folded towel away from drafts to cool. Test seal by pressing lid with your finger. If it stays down when pressed, jar is sealed and may be stored in a cool, dry place indefinitely. If lid pops back up; seal is not airtight and relish should be stored in refrigerator until eaten.

SERVING HINT: Especially good spooned over grilled hot dogs and hamburgers.

FRUIT STUFFING FOR PORK

1/2 cup dried prunes, chopped
1/2 cup dried apricots, chopped
2 cups water
1 1/2 cups soft bread, diced
1 cup apples, peeled, sliced
1/2 cup pears, peeled, sliced
1/2 cup raisins
1/2 cup walnuts, chopped
1/2 tsp salt
1 tsp nutmeg
1/2 tsp allspice
1/2 tsp lemon juice
2 tbsp brown sugar, firmly packed

In saucepan, over high heat, combine water, prunes and apricots, and heat until boiling. Reduce heat to low; simmer 15 minutes or until fruit is tender.

Drain well, and place in bowl. Add the remaining ingredients to the prune-apricot mixture, and mix well.

APPLE-RAISIN BREAD STUFFING

3/4 cup minced onion
1 1/2 cups chopped celery (stalks and leaves)
1 cup butter or margarine
7 cups soft bread cubes
3 cups finely chopped apples
3/4 cup raisins
1 tbsp salt
1 1/2 tsp crushed sage leaves
1 tsp thyme leaves
1/2 tsp pepper

In large skillet, cook and stir onion and celery in butter until onion is tender. Stir in about 1/3 of the bread cubes. Turn into deep bowl. Add remaining ingredients and toss. Stuff meat just before roasting.

May be used for poultry or pork.

Yield: 9 cups (enough for 12-pound turkey)

APPLE 'N BACON CASSEROLE

4 cups cooked, flat wide egg noodles
4 medium cooking apples,
peeled and thinly sliced
1/4 to 1/2 lb bacon, fried and crumbled
4 eggs
2 cups creamed cottage cheese
4 oz cream cheese
2 tbsp brown sugar or honey
2 tsp cinnamon
1 cup breadcrumbs
2 tbsp butter or margarine

Mix noodles, apples and bacon in well-buttered 8-cup casserole dish. In a blender or food processor, combine eggs, cheeses, sugar and cinnamon. Pour over apple mixture and top with breadcrumbs and butter.

Bake in 375°F oven for 30 to 35 minutes.

Makes 4 servings.

VARIATION:

Cooked pork or ham cubes could be used in place of bacon.

PORK TENDERLOIN WITH ONION-APPLE CREAM

1 whole pork tenderloin (about 12 oz)
6 tbsp whipping cream
2 tbsp cream sherry
1 tsp Dijon mustard
1/2 tsp salt
1/2 tsp horseradish
2 tbsp butter
1 large onion, thinly sliced
1 small Golden Delicious apple, thinly sliced
Parsley sprigs

Place the pork on a rack set in a baking pan; insert a meat thermometer into the thickest part and place in a 425°F oven.

Stir together the whipping cream, sherry, mustard, salt and horseradish. Brush mixture over pork frequently during roasting; roast 25 to 30 minutes or until thermometer registers 170°.

Melt the butter in a wide frying pan over medium heat and cook the onion and apple, stirring frequently, until limp and golden (about 20 minutes). Add remaining cream mixture to onion and apple mixture and bring to a boil; place in a small bowl and keep warm.

Arrange pork on a small board or platter and garnish with parsley sprigs. Serve with onion-apple cream to spoon over.

Makes 2 servings.

CHICKEN-APPLE BAKE

5 lb stewing chicken
1/4 cup sweet butter
1/4 cup dry white wine (or 1/4 cup water)
2 tart apples, peeled, cored and sliced
6 ribs of celery with leaves, chopped
1 onion, finely chopped
3 sprigs fresh parsley
1/2 tsp salt
1/4 tsp paprika
2 1/2 tbsp all-purpose flour
2 cups home-made stock or canned chicken broth
1/3 cup sour cream
1 tsp fresh tarragon
Grated Parmesan cheese

Separate chicken into serving pieces. Brown pieces quickly over high heat in butter. Use a pan large enough to eventually hold all the ingredients. Add wine (or water) and remove chicken.

Reduce heat. Add apples, celery, onion, parsley, salt and paprika. Cook gently until tender. Stir in flour and chicken broth. Continue stirring until sauce boils and add chicken. Cover and simmer one hour or until tender.

Remove chicken to a hot, oven-proof serving dish. Strain sauce. Reheat sauce in top of double boiler; over (**not in**) boiling water. Add sour cream, salt and pepper to taste and add tarragon.

Pour sauce over chicken. Sprinkle with grated cheese. Place under broiler until cheese melts.

Serves 6-8.

CREAMY CHICKEN AND APPLES

1 tbsp vegetable oil
4 chicken breast halves
1 medium cooking onion, peeled and sliced
1/2 cup chicken broth
1/4 cup dry white wine
1/4 tsp thyme
1/4 tsp salt
6 medium apples, cored and cut into eighths
1 tbsp all-purpose flour
3/4 cup light cream

Heat oil in frying pan. Saute chicken with onion until golden brown on both sides. Reduce heat and add chicken broth, wine, thyme, and salt. Cover and simmer for 35-40 minutes, until chicken is tender. Remove chicken from pan and keep warm. Add apple slices to pan. Cover and simmer for 3-5 minutes until apples are fork-tender, stirring occasionally.

Dissolve flour in small quantity of cream; add remaining cream. Stir into pan. Cook and stir until slightly thickened. Spoon over chicken.

Makes 4 servings.

NORMANDY APPLE CHICKEN

4 large chicken pieces (total weight 2-3 lbs.)
6 tbsp butter
1 tbsp vegetable oil
1 tbsp all-purpose flour
1/2 cup chicken broth
1/2 cup apple cider
2 tbsp brandy or apple cider
salt and pepper, to taste
4 eating apples
1/2 cup heavy cream

Preheat oven to 375°F.

Heat 2 tbsp of the butter with the oil in a large, heat-proof casserole. Add the chicken pieces and cook for about 5 minutes, turning to brown on all sides. Sprinkle in the flour and stir well.

Pour the broth and cider into the casserole, with the brandy (or apple cider). Season lightly with salt and pepper.

Peel, core and chop 2 of the apples; add to the casserole and bring to a boil. Cover and cook in the oven for 45 minutes, until the chicken is cooked through (the juices will run clear when the chicken is pierced in the thickest part with a fork).

About 10 minutes before the end of cooking time, quarter, peel and core the remaining apples. Heat the remaining butter in a skillet; add the apple quarters and cook gently, turning until golden brown. Transfer to a heat-proof dish. Keep warm in the oven turned down to 225°F.

Using a slotted spoon, transfer the chicken to a warmed serving dish.

Press the remaining contents of the casserole through a strainer to remove lumps and pour into a saucepan. Boil briskly for 3 minutes, then reduce heat and stir in the cream. Heat through gently, then taste and adjust the seasoning if desired.

Pour the sauce over the chicken pieces and garnish with the cooked apple. Serve at once.

Serves 4.

BAKED PORK CHOPS AND APPLES

2 tbsp butter or margarine
6 pork chops
1/2 cup chopped fresh onion
1/2 tsp dried leaf rosemary
3/4 tsp salt
1/8 tsp pepper
3/4 cup water
3 apples, cored and sliced crosswise

In a large skillet melt butter. Add pork chops, 3 at a time and brown well on both sides. Remove chops from skillet. Add onion, rosemary, salt and pepper. Cook 5 minutes until onion is tender. Stir in water. Arrange pork chops and apple slices in a shallow baking dish. Add onion mixture. Cover and bake in a 350°F oven 1 hour, until pork chops are tender.

Makes 6 servings.

APPLE-STUFFED VEAL CHOPS

4 veal chops, each weighing about 1/2 lb, trimmed of excess fat
2 large, tart apples
juice of 1/2 lemon
2 tbsp golden raisins
1 1/2 tsp ground cloves
salt and pepper, to taste
1 tbsp vegetable oil
2 tbsp margarine or butter
2 tbsp golden raisins, soaked in 2 tbsp sherry (optional) to garnish

Using a very sharp knife, make a pocket in each chop. Slit horizontally, from the outside edge to the bone, cutting through to within 1/2" of the bone.

Quarter, peel and core 1 apple. Cut into 1/4" slices and put into a bowl with the lemon juice. Toss the apple slices in the lemon juice, then add the golden raisins and 1 tsp of ground cloves. Mix together well.

Spoon the apple mixture into the pocket of each chop, dividing it equally. Secure the slit edges with wooden toothpicks. Sprinkle the chops with the remaining ground cloves and season with salt and pepper.

Preheat oven to 225°F.

Heat the oil and margarine in a large fry pan; add the veal chops and cook them over high heat for 2 minutes on each side, to brown and seal.

Continued....

Reduce the heat and cook for 10-15 minutes on each side, until cooked through and the juices run clear when the meat is pierced with a sharp knife.

Peel and core the remaining apple. Slice into rings. Using a spatula, transfer the chops to a warmed serving plate and keep warm in the oven. Add the apple rings to the skillet and cook gently until golden brown (turn carefully so that the rings do not break up).

Arrange the cooked apple rings on top of the chops, spoon the golden raisins into the centre of the apple rings and serve.

Serves 4.

VARIATION:

Top with cider sauce.

Pour off excess fat from the skillet after cooking the apples. Pour in 1/2 cup apple cider, then bring slowly to a boil, stirring and scraping the sediment from the bottom of the pan. Add an extra 2 tbsp cider, if necessary. Remove from the heat and stir in 3 tbsp heavy cream. Season to taste. Spoon the sauce over the apples and veal to serve. Serve very hot.

ROAST DUCKLING
WITH APPLE AND SAUSAGE STUFFING

STUFFING:

1/2 lb pork sausage meat
4 or 5 crisp eating apples
1 tbsp granulated white sugar
1/4 tsp cinnamon
1/4 tsp salt
1/4 tsp sage
2 tbsp cognac or brandy
1/4 cup port wine
1/4 cup beef stock or canned beef bouillon

Saute the sausage meat in a frying pan until lightly brown, stirring frequently to break up clumps. Drain well. Retain drained fat.

Peel, quarter and core the apples. Cut each quarter into 2 or 3 lengthwise segments. Saute a few at a time, in the sausage fat. Cook until very lightly browned and almost tender, but still retaining their shape.

Place apples on a platter and sprinkle with the seasonings and cognac or brandy.

Pour the fat out of the frying pan; add the wine and bouillon and boil rapidly until liquid has reduced to 2 or 3 tbsps. Pour over cooked sausage meat.

When both apples and sausages have cooled, mix them delicately together. Stuff loosely into the duck. Sew or skewer the duck and roast it according to the following directions.

Continued....

PREPARING A DUCK FOR ROASTING:

Use only small ducklings, weighing less than 5 lbs.; be sure duckling is well cleaned and plucked.

Pull all loose fat from the cavity and from around the neck. To make carving the breast meat easier, cut out the wishbone. The lower part of the wing is mostly bone; chop it off at the elbow and add it to the stock pot. Ensure that fat glands on the back at the base of the tail have been removed; dig out any yellow residue that may remain, and rub the area with salt and lemon juice.

To minimize fat in meat, prick the skin along the thighs, back and lower part of the breast at 1/2" intervals to allow the inner layer of fat to escape during cooking.

After stuffing the cavity, sew or skewer the legs, wings, and neck skin to the body so the bird will make a neat appearance on the table.

DUCK STOCK:

The neck, heart, gizzard, and lower wings may be used to make stock. Chop into pieces of approximately 1" and brown them in hot oil with 1 chopped onion and 1 chopped carrot.

Pour off fat; add enough liquid to cover the duck parts by about 1/2 inch; use canned beef bouillon or chicken broth, with pinch of parsley, 1/3 bay leaf and 1/8 tsp thyme. Simmer partially covered for 1 1/2 hours or more, skimming fat as necessary. Strain.

NOTE:

When compared to chicken, a duck has more fat, much more bone and much less meat. A 4 1/2 lb bird will only serve 4 people.

TO ROAST:

Medium rare duck will have slightly rosy juice when the meat is pricked.

Well done meat has clear yellow juices.

If your duck is overdone, the meat is brown and dry.

When baking a stuffed 4 1/2 lb duck at 350°F, you will roast approximately 1 hour and 45 minutes for medium rare meat and 2 hours for well done.

DO NOT OVERCOOK!

If your duck is not stuffed, deduct 20 minutes from the cooking times. Note that your duck may wait in the turned-off oven with the door open for about 30 minutes before serving.

SERVING SUGGESTIONS:

Vegetables that will complement your duck include: green peas, broccoli, Brussels sprouts, celery, onion, turnip.

A full red wine will also complement duck.

CURRIED MEATBALLS WITH APPLES

1 lb lean ground beef
1/4 tsp chili powder
2 tbsp chopped parsley (fresh)
1 beaten egg
2 tbsp vegetable oil
1 1/2 large onions, finely chopped
1 celery stalk, finely diced
1 apple, cored, peeled and chopped
2 tbsp curry powder
1 tbsp butter or margarine
2 tbsp flour
1 1/2 cups chicken stock, heated
salt and pepper, to taste
hot pepper sauce (a few drops - to taste)

Place meat, chili powder, half of parsley, egg, some salt and hot pepper sauce into food processor. Blend until meat forms ball. Shape mixture into small meatballs and set aside.

Heat oil in large frying pan. Cook onions, celery, apple and remaining parsley 6-7 minutes over medium heat. Add butter and continue cooking 1 minute.

Place meatballs in pan and cook 5-6 minutes over medium heat, turning meatballs over often.

Sprinkle in flour, mix and continue cooking 2-3 minutes.

Pour in chicken stock and season well. Bring to boil and cook 15 minutes over low heat.

Serve with rice.

TRADITIONAL PORK CHOPS AND APPLES

2 tbsp vegetable oil
4 boneless pork chops, 3/4" thick, trimmed of fat
1 onion, chopped
1 celery stalk, sliced
3 apples, cored, peeled and sliced 1/2" thick
1/2 tsp cinnamon
1 cup chicken stock, heated
salt and pepper, to taste
pinch of ground cloves

Heat oil in large frying pan over medium heat. When hot, add chops and cook 5-6 minutes. Turn pork over, season well and continue cooking 5-6 minutes or adjust time, depending on size of chops. Remove from pan and keep warm.

Add onion and celery to pan; cook 3-4 minutes over medium heat.

Add apples and seasonings; continue cooking 5 minutes. Pour in chicken stock and adjust flavouring to suit your personal taste; cook for an additional 3 minutes.

Pour apples and sauce over pork chops and serve.

Makes 4 servings (approximately 470 calories each).

APPLE-RAISIN OMELET

2 tbsp butter or margarine
2 apples, peeled, cored, sliced
2 tbsp brown sugar
2 tbsp raisins
1 tbsp plum jelly
4 large eggs
2 tbsp light cream
1 tbsp granulated white sugar

Preheat oven to 250°F. Heat 1 tbsp butter in non-stick frying pan. Cook apples and brown sugar, covered, for 4 minutes over medium heat.

Stir in raisins and continue cooking 2 minutes. Add jelly; mix well and finish cooking 3-4 minutes, uncovered. Transfer to oven-proof dish and keep hot in oven.

Heat remaining butter in non-stick frying pan over medium-high heat. Meanwhile, beat eggs and cream together with fork. Pour eggs into hot butter and let cook 30 seconds without stirring.

Gently stir middle of omelet to help eggs set. Continue cooking 30 seconds or until eggs have taken shape but are still soft. Then, using spatula, start rolling omelet from right to left while tilting pan in direction of roll. Sprinkle sugar on underside of omelet to glaze.

Turn omelet out onto heated platter and slit middle open to form pocket. Stuff with some of apple mixture and spoon remainder over omelet. Slice and serve.

SECTION D

PUDDINGS, COBBLERS, & OTHER DESSERTS

APPLE PUDDING

bread crumbs
apples, chopped fine
2 cups brown sugar
1/4 cup butter or margarine
2 tsp cinnamon
1/2 tsp nutmeg

Preheat oven to 350°F.

Fill a casserole dish with a mixture of 1/3 bread crumbs and 2/3 apples (adjust quantities of each to suit the size of your dish).

Mix brown sugar, butter, cinnamon and nutmeg. Spread the sugar mixture over the apple mixture in the dish.

Bake until very brown, approximately 45 minutes.

APPLE PIE PUDDING

2 eggs, beaten
1/4 cup melted butter
1 cup brown sugar
1 cup all-purpose flour
1 tsp baking soda
1/2 tsp cinnamon
1/4 tsp nutmeg
2 cups peeled, chopped apples
nuts and shredded coconut (optional)

Preheat oven to 350°F. Grease a 9" pie pan.

Combine eggs with butter in a medium mixing bowl. Beat in sugar until smooth. Stir in flour, soda, cinnamon and nutmeg. Stir in apples and, if desired, coarsely chopped walnuts or pecans and coconut.

Turn into prepared pan. Bake for about 40 minutes or until toothpick inserted comes out clean.

Cut into wedges and serve warm or cold.

NUTTY APPLE CREAM

6 lb McIntosh apples
(peeled, cored and chopped)
6 tbsp sweet butter
2 tsp lemon rind, grated
6 tbsp honey
2 tbsp unflavoured gelatin
4 tbsp lemon juice
4 tbsp water
6 tbsp dark rum
6 tbsp crystallized ginger,chopped
2/3 cup walnuts, chopped
2 cups heavy cream
1 Red Delicious apple, for garnish.

Place the McIntosh apples in a heavy pot with a tight-fitting cover. Heat slowly, stirring now and then, until apples are quite tender but not too mushy. Check to make sure they are not sticking to the bottom of the pan. (No additional liquid should be needed).

Stir in butter, lemon rind and honey. Continue cooking, uncovered, and stirring until mixture is very thick.

Soak gelatin in 4 tbsp each, water and lemon juice. Stir into hot apple mixture until dissolved. Cool to room temperature.

Stir in rum, ginger and nuts. Chill until mixture begins to thicken again.

Continued....

Whip cream in a separate bowl and fold into apple mixture. Spoon into individual, stemmed dessert dishes and chill well before serving.

To Garnish:

Core the Red Delicious apple and cut it into thin wedges. Place a couple of pieces on top of each dish just before serving.

APPLES BRISTOL

(A cold Apple Dessert served with a Caramel Chip topping)

4 eating apples
peeled rind, and juice of 1 large orange
6 tbsp sugar

Peel, core and cut the apples into quarters. Cut each quarter in half lengthwise.

Add water to orange juice to measure 3/4 cup. Put in a pan with sugar. Heat gently, stirring, until the sugar dissolves, then boil gently for 1 minute. Add the sliced apples; cover and simmer gently for 5 minutes until the fruit is tender. Remove from the heat and leave covered until the mixture is cold.

Cut the orange rind into thin shreds. Put in a small saucepan, cover with cold water and bring to a boil. Boil for 1 minute, then drain and pat dry with paper towels. Place on a saucer, cover and refrigerate.

CARAMEL CHIP TOPPING

1/2 cup brown sugar (lightly packed)
1/2 cup plus 2 tbsp water
vegetable oil, for greasing

Grease a cookie sheet with oil. Put the sugar in a small, heavy-bottomed saucepan with the water, then heat gently, stirring until the sugar has dissolved. Using a dampened pastry brush, brush down the sides of the pan to stop crystals forming.

Continued....

Bring the sugar syrup to a boil and boil for 5 minutes until the syrup turns deep golden.

Immediately remove from the heat and plunge the bottom of the pan into iced water to stop the syrup from cooking any more. Leave for a few minutes until the sizzling stops, then remove from water.

Immediately pour the syrup onto the prepared cookie sheet to form a thin layer. Chill.

Transfer the cold apples to a glass bowl with a slotted spoon, then pour the syrup left over from the apples over the fruit. Scatter the orange rind shreds over the top, then refrigerate for 1 hour.

To serve, crack the set caramel with a rolling pin to form fine chips, then sprinkle over the dish and serve at once before the caramel chips begin to melt into the apples and fruit syrup.

APPLE FLUMMERY

(A particularly light and refreshing dessert - it separates slightly into a shallow layer of liquid at the bottom, topped with a fluffy mixture.)

2 large eggs, separated
1/4 cup white sugar
2 1/2 cups milk
2 tbsp semolina (or other flour)
salt, to taste
1 large, tart apple, weighing about 3/4 lb
  (peeled, cored and pureed)
juice of 1/2 small lemon

TO SERVE:

1 red-skinned eating apple
few drops of lemon juice

Put the egg yolks and sugar in a bowl and beat together until creamy.

Warm milk over moderate heat. Sprinkle in the flour and bring to a boil, stirring. Add salt to taste and reduce the heat, then simmer for 10 minutes, stirring constantly

Gradually stir in the egg yolk and sugar mixture, until well mixed, then continue cooking very gently for a further 2 minutes, stirring all the time. Do not allow it to boil.

Remove the pan from the heat and stir in the apple puree and lemon juice until well blended.

Continued....

Beat the egg whites until stiff and fold into the mixture in the pan.

Carefully spoon the mixture into long-stemmed dessert glasses. Cool for about 30 minutes.

To serve, thinly slice the red-skinned apple, leaving the skin on. Sprinkle with lemon juice to prevent discolouration. Place a few slices on each serving.

Makes 4 servings.

APPLE AND LOGANBERRY WHIP

(A festive, no-bake dessert)

1 lb tart apples, peeled, cored and chopped
1-14 oz can loganberries, *
(drained, with syrup reserved)
2 tbsp white sugar,
(increase or decrease to taste)
3 cups white bread crumbs, lightly toasted
1/2 cup soft light brown sugar
1/4 cup butter or margarine
3/4 cup sour cream
hazelnuts (optional), to decorate

* If you cannot get loganberries, use whole cranberries in syrup

Place the apples in a heavy-bottomed saucepan. Add loganberry syrup, cover and cook gently, stirring occasionally, until the apples are very tender and disintegrating.

Remove from the heat and crush the apples with a wooden spoon or potato masher. Turn the puree into a bowl and stir in the loganberries and sugar, then cool completely.

Meanwhile, mix the bread crumbs with the brown sugar. Melt the butter in a pan, add the crumb mixture and stir over low heat until it turns golden and crisp. Turn into a bowl and cool.

Continued....

Whip the sour cream until thickened (sour cream will whip, but it takes much longer to thicken and form peaks than whipping or heavy cream). Keep in the refrigerator until ready to use.

Spread one-third of the crumbs in the base of a 2-quart glass serving dish. Cover with half the apple mixture and level the surface. Sprinkle over half the remaining crumbs, then add the rest of the apple mixture, followed by a final layer of crumbs.

Carefully spread the whipped sour cream on the top. Decorate with nuts, if desired. Serve as soon as possible.

NOTE: Loganberries have seeds. If you wish to eliminate them, use a wooden spoon to push berries through a fine strainer

RUM-FLAVOURED APPLE ASPIC* - UNMOLDED

(A cold dessert)

*Aspic is defined as a clear jelly used as a garnish

Because the apples for this simple dessert are boiled in a heavy sugar syrup, they jell when chilled and can be unmolded on a serving dish. It makes a pretty effect with its decoration of glaceed fruits. Once made, the aspic may be kept molded or unmolded under refrigeration for at least 10 days.

3 lbs cooking apples
3/4 cup water
3 cups sugar
1 tbsp lemon juice
1 tsp tasteless salad oil
4 oz (about 3/4 cup) glaceed fruits, such as red and green cherries, angelica, orange peel
3 tbsp dark rum

Quarter, core and peel the apples. Cut into lengthwise slices 3/8" thick. You should have about 8 cups. Bring water, sugar and lemon juice to a boil in a heavy enamelled pan. Add the apples and boil over moderately high heat for about 20 minutes, stirring frequently to keep them from sticking and burning. They should become an almost transparent mass.

While apples are cooking, rub inside of a 1-quart cylindrical mold with oil; oil a round of waxed paper and set in the bottom of the mold.

Continued....

with half the glaceed fruits. Dice the rest and add to boil with the apples for 2 to 3 minutes at the end of the cooking.

When apples are done, remove from heat and stir in the rum. Spoon into the mold and chill for 4 to 6 hours, or until set.

Serve as follows:

Surround the mold with a hot towel for 10 to 15 seconds. Run a knife around edge of mold, and turn the aspic onto a chilled serving dish. Surround with "Creme Anglaise" (below) and serve.

Serves 6 to 8.

CREME ANGLAISE

1/2 cup granulated white sugar
4 egg yolks
1 3/4 cups boiling milk
1 tbsp vanilla extract

In a large (3-quart) mixing bowl, gradually beat the sugar into the egg yolks with a wire whip or electric beater and continue beating for 2 to 3 minutes until the mixture is pale, creamy yellow and thickens enough so that when a bit is lifted in the beater, it will fall back into the bowl forming a slowly dissolving ribbon on the surface of the mixture. Do not beat beyond this point or the egg yolks may become granular.

Add the yolk mixture to the milk as follows: While beating the yolk mixture, very gradually pour into the boiling milk in a thin stream of droplets - stir milk mixture frequently. By adding the yolk mixture in this way, the egg yolks are slowly warmed and mixture is creamy.

Pour the mixture into a heavy-bottomed enamelled or stainless steel saucepan and set over moderate heat. Stir slowly and continuously with a wooden spatula or spoon until the sauce thickens just enough to coat the spoon with a light, creamy layer. Do not let the custard come anywhere near a simmer. Maximum temperature should be 165°F on a candy thermometer.

Remove from heat and beat the sauce for a minute or two to cool it. Strain it through a fine sieve* and beat in vanilla.

Set the saucepan in a pan of cold water and stir frequently until cool. Cover and chill until ready to use.

* Old pantyhose, (washed & bleached) make an excellent fine sieve.

VARIATION:

Creme Anglaise may be served warm as well with other desserts.

APPLE COBBLER

(A warm dessert made with cooked apples and covered with golden spoonfuls of biscuit dough - topped with cream)

Preheat oven to 375°F.

BISCUIT DOUGH:

1 1/4 cups all-purpose flour
3 tbsp white sugar
3 tsp baking powder
1/4 tsp salt
1/3 cup shortening
1 egg
1/2 cup milk

Mix together the first 4 ingredients; cut in shortening using pastry cutter or two knives. Using a cup, mix together the milk and egg; add to flour mixture. Stir with fork.

APPLE FILLING:

3 medium apples (peeled, cored and sliced)
1/3 cup white sugar
1 tsp grated lemon rind
3/4 cup water
1/2 tsp cinnamon

Combine all ingredients for filling in saucepan and bring to a boil, stirring until sugar is dissolved. Simmer until apples begin to soften (about 8 minutes).

TO MAKE.

Pour apple mixture into a 1 1/2 quart casserole dish. Drop biscuit dough from a spoon onto hot fruit mixture.

Bake for 25-30 minutes or until light golden.

Serve warm with cream.

VARIATIONS:

Add **raisins** to apple filling.

Make **rhubarb** cobbler by replacing apple filling with rhubarb filling made from 3 cups of cubed rhubarb, 1 cup white sugar and 3/4 cup of water.

Make **peach** cobbler by replacing apple filling with peach filling made from 3 cups of cubed peaches, 1/3 cup white sugar and 3/4 cup of water.

APPLE STRUDEL

DOUGH:

1 tbsp butter
2 tbsp icing sugar
1 egg yolk
2 cups lukewarm water
5 cups all-purpose flour

Blend together the butter, icing sugar and egg yolk. Stir in water. Using electric mixer at medium speed, beat in half of the flour. Then **by hand** blend in the remaining flour.

Knead dough until slightly sticky and bubbles appear. Cut into 6 pieces and shape into round balls. Cover with warm bowl; let stand 15 minutes. Roll each piece of dough to approximately 9" in diameter.

Cream together:

1/2 cup butter
1/2 cup shortening

Divide into 6 portions and spread on each circle of dough.

Stack the circles of dough on a large table covered with a cloth or sheet dusted with flour. Cover with a warm bowl and let stand 30 minutes. Rewarm the bowl occasionally to keep the dough warm.

Pull dough by hand from centre toward the edges. When dough is as transparent as wax paper, cut off thick edges.

The end result will be a piece of dough that will cover the entire table and even hang over the edges.

Let stand for 30 minutes or until dry.

Preheat oven to 375°F.

FILLING:

10 cups apples (peeled and sliced)
1 1/4 cups granulated white sugar
1 tsp cinnamon
1/2 tsp nutmeg

Mix together the sugar and spices.

TO PREPARE STRUDEL:

Cut stretched dough in three equal widths. Mound in a row 1/3 of apples on each portion of dough at table edge. Sprinkle with sugar mixture. Fold over ends of dough to cover apples. Using the table cloth, roll up the three portions of dough - like a jelly roll.

Place on rack in jelly roll pan (or cookie sheet). If desired, cut slits crosswise on strudels to allow steam to escape. Bake for 40-45 minutes until golden brown and apples are tender.

Sprinkle with icing sugar and serve warm.

MAKES 3 STRUDELS.

BRANDIED APPLES FOR DESSERT

2 crisp eating apples
(don't use tart apples; they lose their shape when cooked)
1/4 cup clear honey
3 tbsp sugar
juice of 1 lemon
1/4 cup brandy
lightly whipped cream (to serve)

Peel, core and quarter the apples. Cut each quarter lengthwise into about 3 evenly thick slices.

Put the honey and sugar into a large, heavy-bottomed pan. Gently heat the mixture, stirring occasionally with a wooden spoon, until the sugar has dissolved completely.

Bring to a boil and boil gently until just beginning to smell of caramel. Add the apple slices and turn, using metal spoons, until coated.

Reduce the heat and cook the apple slices gently for about 5 minutes or until all the apples slices are just lightly softened and translucent.

Add the lemon juice, then bring the honey mixture back to a boil.

Tilt the pan slightly to one side and spoon all the juices into a warmed serving pitcher. Keep the juices hot until they are required for serving.

Pour the brandy over the apples and heat through for a few seconds.

Remove the pan from the heat and, using caution, set fire to the brandy.

BE SURE TO AVERT YOUR FACE!

Let the flames die down completely, then serve at once, accompanied by the hot juices and a bowl of lightly whipped cream.
Serves 4.

SECTION E

SPREADS: JAMS, JELLIES, GLAZES

APPLE BUTTER

Apple butter is a fragrant, spicy, semi-soft spread with full flavour that is brought out by slow, even cooking. It's best to make apple butter in a heavy metal pot rather than a thin, light one, in order to maintain an even temperature.

Golden Delicious apples are recommended, however other varieties can be used but the flavour of the apple butter will be sweeter or tarter, depending on the flavour of the fruit (refer to TIPS - 216-218 for other selections of apples).

Ingredients:

4 cups apple juice or cider
12 medium-sized apples (4 lbs)
(peeled, cored and sliced)
1 to 1 1/2 cups brown sugar
2 tsp ground cinnamon

In a heavy 4 or 5 quart pot, bring apple juice to a boil over high heat. Add apples; reduce heat and simmer uncovered, stirring occasionally, for 45 minutes.

Stir in sugar and cinnamon until well blended. Cook uncovered over medium-low heat, stirring occasionally, until mixture is thick and smooth (1 1/2 to 2 hrs).

Continued...

Meanwhile, prepare 5 half-pint canning jars (wash and sterilize by boiling all parts for 15 minutes).

When apple mixture is thick and smooth, fill jars to 1/4" of rim.

Put lid on each jar as it is filled, screwing ring band on as tightly as you comfortably can.

Cool jars away from drafts on a towel, then press lids with your finger. If they stay down, they're sealed and can be stored indefinitely in a cool, dark area. If they do not stay down, seal is not airtight; jelly should be stored in refrigerator and consumed within 1 month.

APPLE-STRAWBERRY JAM

3 1/4 cup crushed strawberries
3/4 cup apple juice
1 package (2 oz) powdered pectin
1 cup light corn syrup
5 1/2 cups granulated white sugar
2 tbsp lemon juice

Place crushed strawberries and apple juice in a 3-quart pan. Stirring vigorously, slowly sprinkle in powdered pectin. Let stand for 30 minutes, stirring occasionally to dissolve pectin completely. Pour in corn syrup and mix well. Gradually stir in sugar. Carefully heat mixture to 100°F (it should be lukewarm and no hotter). When sugar is thoroughly dissolved, stir in lemon juice.

Ladle into 8 sterilized half-pint jars, cover, and freeze for at least 24 hours.

Makes 8 half pints.

SPICY APPLE GLAZE

2/3 cup currant jelly
1/4 cup light corn syrup
1 tbsp cornstarch
1/3 cup apple juice
1/4 tsp cinnamon

Combine all the ingredients in saucepan. Cook, stirring constantly, until sauce is thickened.

Use this delicious glaze to frequently brush over ham during the last 15 minutes of cooking.

Yield: 1 cup

GINGER APPLE PRESERVES

(Use tart apples. These apples are excellent served with meat, with toast or with muffins.)

5 cups granulated white sugar
2 cups water
8 or 9 tart apples
2 tbsp lemon juice
1 jar (5 oz) crystallized ginger

Pour sugar into a heavy 5-quart pot; stir in water until well blended. Bring mixture to a boil over high heat, stirring often. Reduce heat to medium and cook, uncovered for 10 to 15 minutes.

Peel and core apples; cut into 1/4" thick slices to make about 8 cups. Sprinkle with lemon juice; mix well. Drain ginger, reserving syrup, and chop to make about 1/2 cup.

Add apples, ginger and reserved syrup to sugar-water mixture. Cook (boiling gently) over medium heat, stirring occasionally, for 35 to 40 minutes or until preserve is thickened and apples are translucent.

Meanwhile, prepare 6 half-pint canning jars (wash and sterilize by boiling all parts for 15 minutes). Fill jars to 1/8" of rim. Put lid on each jar as it is filled, screwing ring band on as tightly as you comfortably can. Cool jars away from drafts on a towel, then press lids with your finger. If they stay down, they're sealed and can be stored indefinitely in a cool, dark area. If they do not stay down, seal is not airtight; jelly should be stored in refrigerator and consumed within 1 month or so.

HERB-APPLE JELLY

2 cups filtered apple juice
1/4 cup dry thyme leaves
(or substitute 1/3 cup dry basil, 2 tbsp dry rosemary, or 1/4 cup dry mint leaves)
3 tbsp lemon juice
1/4 tsp butter or margarine
3 1/2 cups granulated white sugar
Red or green food colouring (optional)
1 pouch (3 oz) liquid pectin

In 4 or 5 quart pot, heat apple juice to a boil; remove from heat. Stir in thyme; cover and let stand for 30 minutes (2 hours for basil, 15 minutes for rosemary, 10 minutes for mint).

Pour mixture through a "jelly bag" or a cheesecloth-lined strainer*; squeeze out and reserve all the liquid; discard herbs.

Rinse pot and return liquid to pot. Stir in lemon juice, butter, sugar and food colouring (if used). Bring to a boil over high heat, stirring constantly. Add pectin all at once and return to a full rolling boil. Boil for 1 minute, stirring constantly.

Meanwhile, prepare 4 half-pint canning jars (wash and sterilize by boiling all parts for 15 minutes).

* This is another time you can use your old (washed and bleached) pantyhose to strain mixture.

Fill jars to 1/8" of rim. Put lid on each jar as it is filled, screwing ring band on as tightly as you comfortably can.

Cool jars away from drafts on a towel, then press lids with your finger. If they stay down, they're sealed and can be stored indefinitely in a cool, dark area. If they do not stay down, seal is not airtight; jelly should be stored in refrigerator and consumed within 1 month or so.

SECTION F

BEVERAGES

APPLE CIDER PUNCH (HOT)

1 gallon (16 cups) of apple cider
2 tsp whole cloves
2 tsp whole allspice
2 cinnamon sticks (3" long)
2/3 cup granulated white sugar
2 oranges, studded with cloves

Heat cider, cloves, allspice, cinnamon and sugar to boiling; cover and simmer 20 minutes. Strain punch and pour into punch bowl. Float oranges in punch.

32 servings (about 1/2 cup each).

CRANBERRY-APPLE PUNCH (COLD)

3 quarts water
2 cups granulated white sugar
2 cups strong tea
2 cans (6 oz each) frozen lemonade concentrate
2 quarts (8 cups) cranberry cocktail
1 quart (4 cups) apple juice
2 cups orange juice

Heat water and sugar to boiling, stirring constantly until sugar is dissolved. Cool.

Prepare tea, using 3 teaspoons loose tea or 3 teabags and 2 cups boiling water. Cool.

Thaw lemonade. Chill all ingredients. Just before serving, stir together in large punch bowl. Makes 60 servings (about 1/2 cup each).

SPICED CRANBERRY-APPLE CIDER (HOT)

2 quarts (8 cups) apple cider
1 1/2 quart (6 cups) cranberry cocktail
1/4 cup brown sugar (packed)
4 3" cinnamon sticks
1 1/2 tsp whole cloves
1 lemon, thinly sliced

Combine all ingredients in large pot. Heat to boiling; reduce heat and simmer 15 to 20 minutes.

With slotted spoon, remove cinnamon, cloves and lemon slices. If desired, float fresh lemon slice in each cup.

25 servings (about 1/2 cup each).

SECTION G

CANDIES, COOKIES AND SQUARES

CARAMEL APPLES

4 or 5 medium apples
1 pkg (14 oz) caramel candies
(or chocolate caramel candies)
1/2 tsp salt
2 tbsp water
4 or 5 wooden skewers or sticks

Wash 4 or 5 medium apples and dry thoroughly. Remove stem and blossom end of each.

In top of double boiler over hot water, heat 1 package (14 oz) caramel (or chocolate caramel) candies, 1/2 tsp salt and 2 tbsp water, stirring frequently until caramels are melted and mixture is smooth.

Keeping sauce over hot water, place each apple in hot caramel sauce; spoon sauce over apple until it is completely coated. Insert wooden skewer in stem end; remove from sauce and place on waxed paper. Chill until caramel coating is firm.

TAFFY APPLES

12 medium sized red apples
12 wooden meat skewers or sticks

COATING:

3 cups granulated white sugar
1 cup corn syrup
1 cup water
1/2 tsp cinnamon
1/4 tsp red food colouring

Lightly grease a baking sheet.

Wash and dry apples; insert skewers in stem end.

To make coating, combine sugar, syrup and water in saucepan. Heat, stirring constantly, until sugar dissolves. Cover and bring to boil. Boil, uncovered and without stirring, until a few drops in cold water separate into threads (300°F on candy thermometer).

Blend in cinnamon and food colouring. Remove from heat.

Tip saucepan and dip apples in syrup, turning to coat evenly. Place, stick up, on prepared baking sheet to harden.

JUBILEE APPLESAUCE JUMBLES

A very versatile cookie with many variations (see page 83). It's soft, cake-like, caramel coloured.

2 3/4 cups all-purpose flour
1 1/2 cups brown sugar (packed)
1 tsp salt
1/2 tsp baking soda
3/4 cup applesauce
1/2 cup shortening
2 eggs
1 tsp vanilla
1 tsp cinnamon
1/4 tsp cloves
1 cup raisins
1 cup chopped nuts

Preheat oven to 375°F.

Thoroughly mix all ingredients. If dough is soft, cover and chill.

Drop dough by level tablespoons 2" apart onto ungreased baking sheet. Bake 10 minutes or until almost no imprint remains when touched with finger.

Immediately remove from baking sheet; cool.

Spread with Brown Butter Glaze (next page)

Yield: 4 1/2 to 5 dozen cookies

Brown Butter Glaze

1/2 cup butter or margarine
2 cups icing sugar
1 tsp vanilla
2 to 4 tbsp hot water

Heat 1/2 cup butter or margarine over low heat until golden brown. Remove from heat; blend in 2 cups icing sugar and 1 tsp vanilla. Stir in 2 to 4 tbsp hot water until mixture is of spreading consistency.

JUMBLE COOKIE VARIATIONS:

No-Applesauce Jumbles:

Omit applesauce, raisins, cinnamon and cloves. Add 1 cup dairy sour cream.

Coconut Jumbles:

Omit applesauce, raisins, nuts, cinnamon and cloves. Add 1 cup dairy sour cream and 1 cup shredded coconut.

Fruit Jumbles:

Omit applesauce, raisins, nuts, cinnamon and cloves.
Stir in:
- 1 cup dairy sour cream
- 2 cups candied cherries, cut into halves
- 2 cups cut-up dates
- 1 1/2 cups chopped pecans

Drop dough by rounded teaspoons onto ungreased baking sheet. Before baking, place a pecan half on top of each cookie. Omit glaze. Makes about 7 dozen cookies.

Gumdrop Jumbles:

Omit applesauce, raisins, nuts, cinnamon and gloves. and stir in 1 cup dairy sour cream and 4 cups cut-up gumdrops.

Drop dough by tablespoons onto greased and floured baking sheet; bake. Omit glaze. Makes about 6 dozen cookies.

COFFEE APPLE BARS WITH CARAMEL ICING

1/2 cup raisins
1 tbsp dry instant coffee
1/2 cup water
1/2 cup butter
1 tsp vanilla extract
1 cup brown sugar (packed)
1 egg
1 1/2 cups all purpose flour
1 tsp baking powder
1/2 tsp baking soda
1/2 tsp cinnamon
1 grated apple (Granny Smith)

Grease a 9" x 13" baking pan.

MIXTURE A: Combine raisins, coffee and water in saucepan. Bring to boil; remove from heat; cool to room temperature.

Preheat oven to 350°F.

MIXTURE B: Cream butter, vanilla and sugar in small bowl until light and fluffy. Beat in egg until well mixed. Transfer mixture to large bowl.

MIXTURE C: In a separate bowl, combine flour, baking powder, baking soda and cinnamon.

Using large bowl with butter Mixture B, mix in half of wet Mixture A then half of dry Mixture C. Mix well. Mix in the remaining wet ingredients and then the remaining dry ingredients. Mix well. Stir in grated apple.

Spread into greased pan. Bake for about 25 minutes. Spread with Caramel Icing while still hot. Sprinkle with walnuts. Cool in pan before cutting into bars.

CARAMEL ICING

2 tbsp brown sugar
2 tbsp butter
1 tbsp milk
1 cup icing sugar
1/3 cup chopped walnuts

In small saucepan, over low heat, combine sugar, butter and milk; stir constantly until smooth. Do not boil. Gradually stir in icing sugar.

APPLE ALMOND SQUARES

1/2 cup (1/4 lb) butter or margarine
1 cup granulated white sugar
3 eggs
2 cups graham cracker crumbs
1/2 cup all-purpose flour
2 tsp baking powder
1/2 tsp salt
1/2 tsp allspice
2 tsp cinnamon
1 cup milk
2 cups peeled and finely chopped tart apples
(Northern Spy, Idared or Cortland)
3/4 cups chopped blanched almonds
Icing sugar

Preheat oven to 350°F. Grease and flour 9" x 13" baking pan.

MIXTURE A: In a large bowl, beat together the butter and sugar until creamy; add eggs one at a time, beating well after each addition.

MIXTURE B: Stir together the crumbs, flour, baking powder, salt, allspice and cinnamon.

Add dry Mixture B to wet Mixture A. Stir in the apple and almonds until evenly distributed.

Spread batter in prepared baking pan. Bake at 350°F for 35 minutes or until a wooden pick inserted in the centre comes out clean.

Dust with icing sugar just before serving; serve warm or at room temperature. Makes 10 to 12 servings.

APPLE OATMEAL SQUARES

1 cup all-purpose flour
1 cup quick-cooking rolled oats
1/2 cup brown sugar (firmly packed)
1 tsp nutmeg
1/2 tsp salt
3/4 cup butter or margarine
6 medium apples
1/4 cup sunflower seeds

Preheat oven to 375°F. Grease and flour a 9" square baking pan.

Combine flour, oats, sugar, nutmeg and salt. Cut in butter until mixture is crumbly. Measure out 1/2 cup, and set aside for topping. Press remaining oatmeal mixture evenly in bottom of prepared pan.

Peel and core apples; cut in lengthwise halves. Place cut side down on oatmeal base. Add sunflower seeds to reserved crumb mixture and sprinkle over top.

Bake for 40-45 minutes.

Cut into squares and serve warm or cooled.
Makes 12 squares.

SECTION H

CANNING

There are approximately 3 medium apples in 1 pound; 2 1/2-3 lbs. of apples will yield 1 quart of canned fruit.

You may can apples without sweetening, by using just water. Sugar is not needed to prevent spoilage; sugar helps canned fruit hold its shape, colour and flavour. Processing is the same for unsweetened fruit as for sweetened.

NOTE: CAREFULLY FOLLOW WATER-BATH PROCESSING INSTRUCTIONS THAT ACCOMPANIED YOUR CANNING POT.

SWEETENING FRUIT

Apples are best preserved in a light syrup made by heating 4 cups of water with 2 cups of white sugar until sugar is dissolved. Use more sugar if desired. You can use light corn syrup or mild-flavoured honey to replace as much as half the sugar. Do not use brown sugar or molasses.

TO CAN APPLES:

Peel and core apples; cut in pieces. To keep fruit from darkening, drop pieces into water containing 2 tbsp each of salt and vinegar per gallon. Drain, then boil 5 minutes in thin syrup (2 cups of sugar in 4 cups of water) or water.

Pack hot fruit in glass jars to 1/2" from top. Cover with hot syrup or water, leaving 1/2" space at top of jar. Place lids on jars; process in boiling water bath (15 minutes for pint jars, 20 minutes for quart jars).

As soon as you remove jars from canner, tighten lids to complete seal.

Cool jars away from drafts on a towel, then press lids with your finger. If they stay down, they're sealed and can be stored indefinitely in a cool, dark area. If they do not stay down, seal is not airtight; jelly should be stored in refrigerator and consumed within 1 month.

TO CAN APPLESAUCE:

Make applesauce, sweetened or unsweetened according to your preference (refer to Section B, page 16-19 for instructions).

Heat to simmering; stir to keep from sticking.

Pack hot applesauce in glass jars to 1/4" from top. Place lids on jars; process in boiling water bath for 10 minutes (for both pints and quarts).

As soon as you remove jars from canner, tighten lids to complete seal.

Cool jars away from drafts on a towel, then press lids with your finger. If they stay down, they're sealed and can be stored indefinitely in a cool, dark area. If they do not stay down, seal is not airtight; jelly should be stored in refrigerator and consumed within 1 month.

SECTION I

FREEZING

FREEZING APPLES

Syrup pack is preferred for apples to be used for fruit cocktail or uncooked dessert. Apples packed in sugar or frozen unsweetened are good for pie-making. For better quality, apple slices need to be treated (with lemon juice or vinegar/salt/water) to prevent darkening (refer to Section P - Tips for specific instructions).

Select full-flavoured apples that are crisp and firm, not mealy in texture. Wash, peel and core; slice medium apples into twelfths, large ones into sixteenths. Pack in one of the following ways:

SYRUP PACK

Use a light syrup (water mixed with 40-50% sugar - 1/2 cup sugar for every cup of water). For a better quality frozen product, add 1/2 tsp crystalline ascorbic acid* to each quart of syrup.

*(Vitamin C - available from your pharmacy in the vitamin section)

Slice apples directly into cold syrup in freezer container; starting with 1/2 cup syrup to a pint container. Press fruit down in containers and add enough syrup to cover. Leave room for the fruit to expand when frozen ("head" space). Seal and freeze.

Continued....

SUGAR PACK:

If you plan to use your apples in pies or other recipes where the their appearance is not important you can freeze them without pre-treating to prevent darkening of fruit.

Over each quart (1 1/4 pounds) of apple slices, sprinkle evenly 1/2 cup sugar (white or brown) and stir. Pack apples into containers and press fruit down, leaving head space. Seal and freeze.

HINT: If you are planning to use your apples for pies, follow the directions for "sugar pack", add your cinnamon and nutmeg when stirring in sugar. Use "freezer bags" to store apples ; fill each bag with enough apples for one pie. Place your bags in aluminum pie plate so that bag takes the shape of plate. Freeze. When apples are removed from freezer, they are in a bag in the shape of a pie and can be placed in an unbaked pie shell without thawing. Allow an extra 10 minutes baking time.

IF APPEARANCE OF APPLES IS IMPORTANT:

To prevent darkening of apples during preparation, slice them into a solution of salt/vinegar/water (refer to Section P - Tips for specific instructions). Hold apples in this solution no more than 15 to 20 minutes. Drain.

To further retard darkening, place slices in a single layer in steamer; steam 1 1/2 to 2 minutes. Cool in cold water; drain.

Follow directions for SUGAR PACK.

UNSWEETENED PACK:

Follow directions for sugar pack, omitting sugar.

FREEZING APPLESAUCE

Select full-flavoured apples. Prepare applesauce according to recipe of your choice. Cool. Pack into containers, leaving head room, and freeze.

SECTION J

CRAFTS

SPICED CENTREPIECE

Tie bundles of cinnamon sticks with tartan ribbon; nestle in among pine cones and shiny red apples in a basket or wooden bowl for a warm "country" centrepiece.

FESTIVE GARLANDS

Garlands can be made by threading sliced apples, bay leaves, cranberries, hot red peppers (dried), and drilled nutmegs onto a length of red ribbon.

Finish the end with a double-knotted loop to allow for easy hanging.

DRIED APPLE-RING WREATH

13-15 large apples (preferrably Red Delicious*)
2 cups reconstituted lemon juice
3 tbsp salt
3 tbsp citric acid
large wire cake rack
12" double wire wreath or other wreath form
florists' wire
hot glue gun

* Red Delicious apples are best because their skin is deepest in colour and the colour is retained even after drying.

Pre-heat oven to the lowest setting available.

Mix the lemon juice, salt and citric acid in a large bowl. Then cut the apples cross-wise into about 1/4" slices, saving only those pieces which have the star-shaped pattern formed by the seeds. Soak the apples in the lemon mixture for approximately five minutes.

Drain the apples on paper towels and then lay them on the wire cake racks. Place them in the pre-heated oven and leave them to dry out for six to eight hours. By this stage, they should be very leathery and may be slightly curled at the edges.

If you are going to hang your wreath, at this stage, form a hanging loop on the back of the wire wreath using florists' wire.

Divide the slices into two piles - one pile for the most attractive pieces which you will use for the front of the wreath, and the other for the less-than-perfect ones you can use for the back. Using the hot glue gun, lay the slices around the wreath, overlapping them as you go.

Once dry, gently turn the wreath over and repeat the process on the other side. You may glue as many layers of apples as you feel required to cover the wreath form.

Bows, cinnamon sticks, aniseed stars and other spices can be added to this wreath, but it looks very attractive even without them.

APPLE-HEAD DOLLS

Dried apples take on a wrinkled, leathery appearance that suggests the skin of elderly farmers, fishermen or others who have been exposed to wind and sun for many years.

It will take several weeks to make each head.

Although there are many ways of making bodies for the dolls, the heads are made in much the same way by all doll makers.

Use a firm, dry apple - MacIntosh are too juicy, but Golden Delicious or other hard winter apples work well. Peel the apple, leaving stem and blossom and a little peeling around each. Rinse well in cold water and dry.

Using a wooden stick (toothpick, skewer or orange stick - **NOT** a steel knife blade), make a slit in the apple where you want the mouth to be. Turn the corners up or down or make the line straight, but make it deeper toward the centre. The slit should be about 1/4" deep. Make "dimples" by making rounded slits at each corner of the mouth slit.

You may carve the rest of the features of the face or "mold" them as the apple dries. The apple will shrink to about half its original size when dry so be sure to take this into consideration and space out any carving you do.

Soak the apple for an hour in pure lemon juice (you may freeze your container of juice for re-use when making more dolls).

Put a long piece of wire through the core and make loops at either end. Hang the apple in an airy spot, out of the sun, and let it dry for two or three days. If you have carved the features, you may be able to just let it dry of its own accord; if you have just made slits, you can begin forming the face as the apple dries.

Use the eraser end of a pencil (or similar object) and begin pushing carefully to form features. Push in for eyes and around the nose. Do this gently; it takes several weeks to work on each head and it is better to do a little each day until the features begin to take shape.

You may find that you have to make a tiny cut above the mouth for the bottom of the nose. Push the eye sockets toward the centre to form a ridge for the bridge of the nose, pinch the cheeks to form the hollows beside the nose.

Push upward from the eye socket and down from the forehead to form brows.

By working slowly, you can form more character in the face and have more natural-looking features.

AFTER ABOUT A MONTH THE APPLE SHOULD BE DRY.

Continued....

HANDS:

If your doll is to have "apple" hands, you should make these when you begin the head. Cut apple in half and then in several slices, soak in lemon juice and hang on thread to dry. When they have dried enough to be cut with scissors, make snips for the four fingers and cut a wedge out to form the thumb. As they dry, form the fingers by pinching and separating them.

If you make several hands, you will have a better chance of getting a good, evenly matched pair.

BODY:

The body of your doll will often be determined by the appearance of the head.

Pull the wire so that the top loop is against the head. Bend the loop down flat so it can be covered with hair. A drop of white glue at the loop end will help hold the head in place. Make a small bend in the wire below the head, or a tiny loop, just to hold the head in place. This will be covered later by the body.

Cut another wire, the length of both arms, and twist it around the body wire. Now loop the body wire around it so neither can slip. Keeping the body in proportion with the head, bend the wire at the hip and again at the foot, doubling wire back to the hip and down again to form the other leg.

An alternative method is to use a double wire all along, pushing both ends through the head and hanging the drying apple from the resulting loop. In this way, the arms can be formed from the main wire. Using a double wire this way will make a stronger doll, but apple-head dolls are more for decoration and show and are not necessarily subjected to much strain.

Wrap the wire with strips of nylon stocking or other material (note that none of the wrapped wire will show on the finished doll). Extra padding or wrapping fills out the body.

Once the form is made and wrapped, arms and legs can be bent to any position.

If the single wire was used, hands may be attached by sticking the wire into the wrists. If the double-wire method was used, make a small slit in the wrist to push the loop into. In either case, secure with a drop of white glue.

Many craft shops carry supplies to finish your dolls. You will find hair, miniature glasses, hats, and even miniature pets. Or, you can be creative and make them yourself.

Dressing the doll can be at your own whim or fancy. Use solids or miniature calico and gingham prints. Well-worn denim will be soft enough for overalls. Wide lace can be a shawl or a dressy apron for a grannie. Tiny leftover pieces of trims can be glued or stitched to the wrists for cuffs.

Continued....

Felt or worn-out kid gloves can be made into shoes or boots.

Raw wool makes perfect hair, since its colour and texture are appropriate for the wrinkled skin of the face. It can be wrapped around, braided or just glued on in disarray. Strips of it can be glued in place for bushy eyebrows or mustaches and beards.

The face can be accented by using tiny beads tucked into the eyes, a faint touch of pink on the cheeks and a dot of red on the mouth.

Clothing and accessories can be made in many ways. A fisherman could have a little knit cap, a woodsman could have an axe which could be made of wood; a housewife or witch could have a broom made of cornhusks or grass tied to a small stick.

Sweaters can be made from worn-out stockings, eyeglasses from fine wire, jewellery from small beads. Little bouquets of dried flowers or herbs can be carried in bundles or baskets. Knitting needles can be made from toothpicks with miniature knitting on them.

You are only limited by your imagination!

SECTION K

PIES, CRISPS AND CRUMBLES

BAKING TIPS - PIES

- Roll pastry dough on a floured board or cloth.
- As rolling proceeds, lift pastry occasionally to make sure it is not sticking to cloth or board. If pastry sticks, loosen with a long, flexible metal spatula and re-flour surface before resuming rolling.
- Pastry should be rolled to about 1/8" thickness. To measure correct size of rolled pastry circle, turn pie plate upside down over pastry. Pastry should be 1 1/2" larger than edge of pie pan.
- Pies are best served the day they are baked.
- Using ready-made pastry shells can save you a lot of time. These can be purchased in the frozen food section of grocery stores or stores that specialize in frozen foods.
- Use the ready-made tart shells to make miniature "uncovered" pies. Top with whipped cream or ice cream.

CLASSIC PIE CRUST

2 cups all-purpose flour
1 tsp salt
2/3 cup plus 2 tbsp solid vegetable shortening
1/4 cup ice water

In a medium mixing bowl mix flour and salt. Cut in shortening with a pastry blender or two knives until the particles resemble giant peas. Sprinkle with water, a little at a time, mixing lightly with fork, until all flour is moistened. Make a ball with the dough and place on a lightly floured cloth-covered board.

Divide dough in half. Roll out into 12" circle. Fold pastry in half and carefully transfer to 9" pie plate. Unfold and loosely place pastry in pan, leaving an overhang.

Fill pie shell with desired filling.

For top crust, roll remaining half of dough large enough to extend 1" beyond edge of pan. Fold pastry for top crust in quarters. Moisten edge of bottom crust with water. Place folded pastry over pie. Unfold. Fold edge of top pastry under edge of lower pastry on rim. Seal by pressing with fingertips; flute. Make several slits near centre to allow for steam to escape.

GRANDMA'S PIE CRUST

2 1/2 cups all-purpose flour
1 cup shortening
1 egg
dash salt
2-3 tbsp vinegar
water

Mix flour, salt and shortening; cut with pastry blender or two knives until crumbly and evenly mixed. Mix together egg, vinegar and enough water to measure 1/2 cup. Stir into flour mixture.

Knead lightly. **THE LESS YOU HANDLE THE DOUGH, THE MORE FLAKY IT WILL BE.**

Divide into 4 parts. Makes 4 one-crust pie shells or 2 two-crust pies (2 bottoms and 2 tops). Roll out as in "Classic" Pie Crust recipe.

To bake one-crust shells: prick at frequent intervals with fork (to prevent bubbling) and bake at 400°F for 10-15 minutes or until golden. The prepared crust can then be filled with ready-to-eat fillings.

For two-crust pies, add filling and bake according to directions in recipe for filling.

To avoid excessive browning and prevent spills in your oven, you can generally baked your filled pies at 400°F for 15 minutes and then reduce heat to 350° and continue baking for 45 minutes or until filling is done.

Continued...

To make your pie crusts golden brown and attractive, brush with egg white or condensed milk before baking.

APPLE PIE

8" Pies

Pastry for 8" two-crust pie
1/2 cup brown sugar (lightly packed)
3 tbsp flour
1/4 tsp nutmeg
1/4 tsp cinnamon
Dash salt
5 cups thinly sliced peeled tart apples
1 tbsp butter or margarine

9" Pies

Pastry for 9" two-crust pie
3/4 cup brown sugar (lightly packed)
1/4 cup flour
1/2 tsp nutmeg
1/2 tsp cinnamon
Dash salt
6 cups thinly sliced peeled tart apples
2 tbsp butter or margarine

10" Pies

Pastry for 10" two-crust pie
1 cup brown sugar (lightly packed)
1/3 cup flour
1 tsp nutmeg
1 tsp cinnamon
Dash salt
8 cups thinly sliced peeled tart apples
3 tbsp butter or margarine

Continued...

Preheat oven to 425°F. Prepare pastry. Stir together sugar, flour, nutmeg, cinnamon and salt; mix with apples. Turn into pastry-lined pie pan; dot with butter. Cover with top crust which has slits cut in it; seal and flute. Cover edge with 2-3" strip of aluminum foil to prevent excessive browning; remove foil last 15 minutes of baking.

Bake 40-50 minutes or until crust is golden.

VARIATIONS:

Apple-Cheese Pie: Follow recipe for 9" pie except - pour half the apple mixture into pastry-lined pie pan; cover with 5 slices (1 ounce each) process cheddar cheese and top with remaining apples.

Apple-Pecan Pie: Follow recipe for 10" pie except - stir in 2/3 cup chopped pecans with the sugar. Increase baking time to 50-60 minutes; spread hot pie with Crunchy Pecan Glaze.

To make Crunchy Pecan Glaze: in small saucepan, combine 1/4 cup brown sugar (packed), 1/3 cup chopped pecans and 2 tbsp light cream. Cook over low heat, stirring constantly, until mixture is of glaze consistency.

Canned Apple Pie: Follow recipe for 9" pie except - substitute 2 cans (20 oz. each) apple slices, drained, for the fresh apples or use prepared apple pie filling.

Dutch Apple Pie: Follow the recipe for 9" pie except make extra large slits in top crust; 5 minutes before pie is completely baked, pour 1/2 cup whipping cream through slits in top crust and bake 5 minutes. Best served warm.

French Apple Pie: Prepare pastry for 9" one-crust pie; omit butter and top apple filling with Crumb Topping: Mix 1 cup flour, 1/2 cup firm butter or margarine and 1/2 cup brown sugar (packed) until crumbly. Bake 50 minutes. Cover topping with foil for last 10 minutes of baking if top browns too quickly. Best served warm.

Green Apple Pie: Follow recipe for 9" pie except - increase sugar to 1 1/4 cups and use green apples.

CLASSIC FRESH APPLE PIE

Pastry for 9" two-crust pie
1 cup brown sugar (lightly packed)
1 tsp cinnamon
1 tsp nutmeg
7 1/2 cups thinly sliced, peeled green apples

Preheat oven to 350°F. Combine cinnamon, nutmeg and sugar and mix thoroughly with apples. Turn into pastry-lined pan. Trim off overhanging edges. Cover with top crust and seal edges.

Bake for 50 minutes until pastry is well browned.

APPLE CUSTARD PIE

Pastry for one-crust pie
1/3 cup butter or margarine
1/3 cup brown sugar (lightly packed)
3 egg yolks
2 cups applesauce
1 tbsp lemon juice
dash nutmeg
dash cinnamon

Cream butter and sugar. Beat the yolks of 3 eggs and add to butter mixture. Stir in applesauce and flavourings. Cook in an unbaked pie shell for 35 minutes at 350°F.

Add meringue, brown and serve.

MERINGUE:

3 egg whites
3/4 cup granulated white sugar
1/8 tsp salt

Using a narrow bottom, glass bowl, beat egg whites until they hold soft peaks. Beating continuously, add sugar and salt gradually. Continue to beat 1 minute after sugar has been added.

Spoon meringue over pie, bake at 400°F for approximately 5 minutes - until golden brown.

To increase volume of meringue, increase the number of egg whites and the amount of sugar.

GREEN APPLE PIE (Bottomless)

Green apples, peeled, sliced
(number determined by the size of dish you use - ingredients shown are for 8" pan)
2/3 cup granulated white sugar
1/4 tsp salt
1 tsp cinnamon
1/2 tsp nutmeg
2 heaping tsps butter or margarine
pastry for top of pie (see pastry recipe)

Optional: 1/4 cup cranberries, sprinkling of dried raisins.

Preheat oven to 400°F. This dessert can be either a shallow pie or a deep-dish pie. Grease the pan of your choice.

Prepare sufficient apples to fill to overflowing (allowing for shrinkage) the pan or dish you plan to use. Spread apples in greased pan.

Mix together white sugar, salt, cinnamon and nutmeg. Sprinkle over the apples and dot with butter. Cover with pastry and slit at the centre to allow steam to escape.

Bake at 400°F for 15 minutes to brown. Reduce heat to 350° and continue baking for 45 minutes. Serve hot.

VARIATIONS:

Adding cranberries to apples will add a delicious touch of colour. Raisins will also add a delicious touch.

CRAN-APPLE PIE

Tart and sweet, colourful pie with delicate combination of apple, orange and cranberry flavours.

Pastry for 9" two-layer pie
3 tbsp cornstarch
2 tbsp granulated white sugar
2 tsp grated orange peel
1 can (16 oz.) whole cranberry sauce
1 can (20 oz.) apple slices, drained
 or 3 cups fresh, peeled, sliced apples
1 tbsp butter or margarine

Preheat oven to 425°F.

Mix cornstarch, sugar, orange peel and cranberry sauce in saucepan. Heat to boiling over medium heat, stirring constantly. Boil and stir 1 minute. Gently stir in apples; set aside.

Prepare pastry. Spread cranberry-apple mixture in pastry-lined pie pan; dot with butter. Cover with top crust which has slits cut in it; seal and flute. Cover edge with 2-3" strip of aluminum foil to prevent excessive browning; remove foil last 10 minutes of baking. Bake 40 minutes or until crust is brown.

FRESH CRANBERRY-APPLE PIE

Pastry for 9" two-crust pie
1 3/4 to 2 cups brown sugar (lightly packed)
1/3 cup all-purpose flour
3 cups sliced peeled tart apples
    (2 to 3 medium)
2 cups fresh or frozen cranberries
2 tbsp butter or margarine

Preheat oven to 425°F. Prepare pastry. Stir together sugar and flour. In pastry-lined pan, alternate layers of apples, cranberries and sugar mixture, beginning and ending with apple layers; dot with butter.

Cover with top crust which has slits cut in it; seal and flute. Cover edge with 2-3" strip of aluminum foil to prevent excessive browning; remove foil last 15 minutes of baking. Bake 40-50 minutes or until crust is brown. Cool.

DEEP DISH APPLE PIE

Pastry for 9" one-crust Pie
1 1/2 cups brown sugar (lightly packed)
1/2 cup all-purpose flour
1 tsp nutmeg
1 tsp cinnamon
1/4 tsp salt
12 cups thinly sliced peeled apples
(about 10 medium)
2 tbsp butter or margarine

Preheat oven to 425°F.

Stir together sugar, flour, nutmeg, cinnamon and salt; mix with apples. Turn into ungreased square pan, 9"x 9"x 2"; dot with butter.

Prepare pastry; roll into 10" square. Fold pastry in half; cut slits near centre. Unfold over fruit in pan; fold edges under just inside edge of pan.

Bake 1 hour or until juice begins to bubble through slits in crust. Best served warm.

APPLE-MINCEMEAT CRUMBLE

4 cups peeled, sliced apples (about 5 medium)
1 1/2 cups mincemeat
2 tbsp lemon juice
1/2 cup all-purpose flour
1/2 cup chopped Brazil nuts
1/3 cup packed brown sugar
1/3 cup rolled oats
1/3 cup butter or margarine

Preheat oven to 375°F.

In 9" square pan, combine apples, mincemeat and lemon juice. In medium bowl, stir together flour, nuts, sugar and oats. Cut in butter until crumbly. Sprinkle evenly over apple mixture.

Bake for 45 minutes or until apples are tender.

Serve warm with ice cream. Serves 6.

APPLE-MINCEMEAT PIE

Pastry for 9" one-crust pie
1/4 cup all purpose flour
1/3 cup granulated white sugar
1/8 tsp salt
1 tbsp butter
1/4 cup water
2 tbsp red cinnamon candies
1 jar (18 oz.) prepared mincemeat (approx. 2 cups)
3 tart apples

Preheat oven to 425°F.

Prepare pastry. Spread mincemeat in pastry-lined pie pan and sprinkle with 2 tbsp of the flour.

Mix remaining flour, the sugar, salt and butter until crumbly.

Heat water and cinnamon candies, stirring until candies are dissolved; set aside.

Peel apples and cut into quarters. Cut quarters into wedges, 1/2" thick at outer side. Cover mincemeat with 2 circles of overlapping apple wedges; sprinkle with sugar mixture. Spoon cinnamon syrup over top, moistening as much of sugar mixture as possible.

Cover edge of pastry with 2-3" strip of aluminum foil to prevent excessive browning; remove foil last 15 minutes of baking. Bake 40 to 50 minutes.

APPLE CRUMBLE PIZZA PIE

Pastry for 9" two-crust pie
6 to 7 tart apples
1/2 cup brown sugar (lightly packed)
1 tsp cinnamon
1/4 tsp nutmeg

Preheat oven to 450°F.

Prepare pastry and roll 1" larger than 12- or 13" pizza pan. Ease into pizza pan; flute edge.

Do not peel apples; cut into slices, about 1/2 inch thick (about 8 cups). Beginning at edge of crust and overlapping slices, cover crust with apples.

Stir together sugar, cinnamon and nutmeg; sprinkle over apple slices. Top with Crumble Topping (below).

Bake 30 to 40 minutes or until edge is golden brown and apples are tender. Best served warm and, if desired, topped with cinnamon ice cream.

8 to 10 servings.

CRUMBLE TOPPING

Mix 3/4 cup all-purpose flour, 1/2 cup sugar and 1/2 cup firm butter or margarine until crumbly.

CHRISTMAS FRUIT PIE

Pastry for 10" two-crust pie
1 cup pitted prunes
2/3 cup candied kumquats
or 223 ml bottle kumquats
4 cooking apples
10 oz marzipan, at room temperature
1/4 cup butter or margarine, at room temperature
2 eggs
1 tbsp all-purpose flour
1 egg yolk
1 tsp water

Preheat oven to 425°F.

Place prunes in a medium-size bowl. Cover with 1 1/2 cups boiling water. Let stand 10 minutes.

Meanwhile, roll pastry into a 15" round. Place pastry in a 10" pie plate. Do not trim overhanging pastry as it will be used to cover pie. Set pie plate aside while preparing filling.

Drain prunes well, then coarsely chop. Place in a medium-size bowl. Drain kumquats, setting aside 2 tbsps syrup. Quarter kumquats and place in bowl with prunes. Peel and core whole apples, then slice into 1/4" rings. They will measure about 3 cups. Place in bowl with prunes and kumquats. Stir until combined.

Continued...

Place crumbled marzipan in a food processor. Combine with 1/4 cup butter, using an on-and-off motion, until smooth. With motor running, add 1 egg at a time, mixing well after each addition.

Turn marzipan mixture into prepared pie shell, spreading evenly over bottom of shell. Toss fruit mixture with 2 tbsp reserved kumquat syrup, then with flour. Spoon over marzipan mixture.

Fold excess pastry over filling, letting it fall where it may. It will have a casual, draped appearance. In small bowl, stir yolk with water. Brush over pastry.

Bake pie on lower rack of preheated 425°F oven for 12 to 15 minutes or until pastry edges begin to turn golden. Then reduce oven temperature to 350°F and bake for 55 to 60 minutes more or until crust is golden brown. Cool on a wire rack. Serve warm or at room temperature. Pie will keep well for 3 or 4 days. It also freezes well.

Makes 10 servings

CREAMY DUTCH APPLE DESSERT

1/4 cup butter or margarine
1 1/2 cups graham cracker crumbs
1 14-oz can Eagle Brand sweetened condensed milk
1 cup sour cream
1 cup lemon juice
4 cups peeled and sliced apples

TOPPING:

1/4 cup chopped walnuts
1/2 tsp ground cinnamon

Preheat oven to 350°F.

In a 1 1/2 quart shallow baking dish (10"x 6"); melt butter in oven. Sprinkle in crumbs; stir well. Press on bottom of dish.

In medium bowl, mix milk, sour cream and lemon juice; spread evenly over crumbs.

Spoon apples evenly over creamy layer.

Bake 25-30 minutes or until set. Cool slightly.

TOPPING:

In small dish, mix nuts and cinnamon; sprinkle over pie filling. May be served hot or cold. Refrigerate leftovers.

Continued...

VARIATIONS:

Omit cinnamon

Substitute blueberry, peach or cherry filling for apples.

Place creamy filling in ready-to-use frozen tart shells; top with nut mixture; bake 25-30 minutes.

DOUBLE-DECKER APPLE PIE

Preheat oven to 450°F. Prepare sufficient pastry for two pies.

Line one 9" pie plate with a circle of aluminum foil so there is a 1" overhang at the edge.

Melt together: 3 tbsp butter, 1/2 cup lightly packed brown sugar. Pour into prepared pie plate.

On top of butter/sugar mixture, arrange an attractive assortment of red and green candied cherries.

Roll out pastry and line a second pie plate; trim.

Roll out two top crusts.

PIE FILLING:

12 cups sliced apples (peeled)
1 cup granulated white sugar
1/4 cup all-purpose flour
1 tsp cinnamon
1/2 tsp nutmeg

Toss ingredients for filling together and place half of apple mixture in each pie plate. Arrange apples in an attractive pattern in the foil-lined pie plate.

Cover with top crusts; seal and flute edges; slit or prick tops to allow steam to escape.

Continued...

Bake both pies at 450°F for 15 minutes or until pastry is golden. Reduce heat to 350°F and continue baking 30-35 minutes longer. Cool to lukewarm.

Invert foil-lined pie over two crust pie. Remove plate and foil.

Serve warm with whipped cream or vanilla ice cream.

DUTCH APPLE PIE

Pastry for 9" one-crust pie
1 1/4 cups lightly packed brown sugar
1/2 cup all purpose flour
1 tsp cinnamon
1/3 cup butter or margarine
6 apples, peeled, cored and quartered
1/4 cup whipping cream

Preheat oven to 425°F.

Prepare pastry. Roll and line 9" pie plate.

Combine brown sugar, flour and cinnamon. Cut in butter until crumbly. Spread 1/3 of sugar mixture in prepared pastry. Fit apples tightly in single layer in pie shell. Sprinkle remaining sugar mixture over apples. Pour cream over top.

Bake at 425°F for 15 minutes, then reduce temperature to 350°F and bake 20-30 minutes longer or until apples are tender. Serve warm or cool.

Makes 6 to 8 servings.

SNOW-TOPPED APPLE PIE

Preheat oven to 425°F.

Prepare pastry; roll out dough and line a 9" pie plate. Flute edge and prick pastry several times to prevent bubbling. Bake in preheated oven for 10 to 12 minutes or until golden. Cool.

FILLING:

In a large saucepan, combine:

3/4 cup maple syrup
1/4 cup water
7 cups apples (peeled, sliced)

Bring to boil, cover and simmer until apples are just tender (8-10 minutes); stirring occasionally. Drain, reserving syrup.

Meanwhile, in a saucepan, melt 2 tbsp butter or margarine and stir in 1/4 cup all-purpose flour. Add reserved syrup and cook, stirring constantly, until thickened. Pour over drained apples and turn into prepared pie shell. Cool.

TOPPING:

2 (4-oz) packages of cream cheese (softened)
1 1/2 cups icing sugar
2-3 tbsp milk
1 tsp vanilla

Beat together until fluffy. Swirl on cooled pie and garnish with unpeeled apple wedges dipped in lemon juice.

APPLE TOPSY TURVY (Upside Down Pie)

1 cup all-purpose flour
1 tbsp baking powder
1/4 tsp salt
1/2 cup rolled oats
2 1/2 tbsp light brown sugar
1 1/4 cups margarine or butter
(cooled and chopped to small bits)

FILLING:

1 2/3 cups peeled and chopped tart apples
1/2 cup mincemeat

Preheat oven to 375°F. Grease a 7" glass pie plate.

Sift the flour, baking powder and salt into a bowl, then stir in the oats and sugar. Add the margarine and rub it into the mixture with your fingertips. Set aside.

To make the filling; mix the apples in a bowl with the mincemeat.

Spoon 1/3 of the oat mixture into the prepared pie plate and press evenly over the base. Cover with half the mincemeat mixture. Add another layer of oat mixture and cover with the remaining mincemeat mixture. Press the rest of the oat mixture evenly over the top.

Bake for about 1 hour, until the surface is lightly browned and the dessert is just shrinking from the sides of the pie plate.

Continued...

Carefully turn upside-down onto a serving plate so that it is "topsy-turvy" with the base becoming the top. Serve hot or warm.

APPLE CRISP - VERSION 1.

(Our Favourite Version of this Recipe)

4 cups sliced, peeled tart apples
(about 4 medium - we like to use Cortland)
2/3 to 3/4 cup brown sugar (packed)
1/2 cup all-purpose flour
1/2 cup rolled oats (quick cooking)
3/4 tsp cinnamon
3/4 tsp nutmeg
1/3 cup butter or margarine, softened.

Preheat oven to 375°F. Grease square pan, 8"x 8"x 2". Place apple slices in pan. Mix remaining ingredients thoroughly. Sprinkle over apples.

Bake 30 minutes or until apples are tender and topping is golden brown. Serve warm alone or with light cream or ice cream.

6 servings

VARIATION:

Cherry Crisp - substitute 1 can cherry pie filling for the apples; use lesser amount of sugar.

APPLE CRISP - VERSION 2
(Not So Humble Pie)

6 apples (Use McIntosh, Cortland, Golden Delicious, Northern Spy or Idared)
2 tbsp brown sugar
1/2 tsp cinnamon
1/8 tsp nutmeg
1/8 tsp ginger
1/2 cup butter or margarine

1 9" unbaked pie shell
1/2 cup whole wheat flour
1/2 cup oatmeal
1/2 cup brown sugar
1/4 cup wheat germ

Peel, core and slice apples.

Preheat oven to 425°F.

Combine sugar, cinnamon, nutmeg and ginger. Sprinkle over apples and toss to coat thoroughly. Arrange in pie shell.

TOPPING: Combine whole wheat flour, oatmeal, brown sugar and wheat germ. Cut butter into mixture, using a pastry blender, until butter pieces are size of small peas. Spoon topping evenly over apples. Bake pie at 425°F for 10 minutes. Lower oven temperature to 375°F.

For McIntosh, Cortland and Northern Spy apples, bake an additional 30 to 40 minutes.

For Golden Delicious and Idared apples, bake an additional 40 to 50 minutes.

APPLESAUCE CRISP VERSION 3

1 1/2 to 2 cups applesauce (sweetened)
pinch ground nutmeg
1/4 cup raisins
2/3 cup crushed bread crumbs
3 tbsp butter or margarine

Pour applesauce into a shallow, greased baking pan and dust top lightly with nutmeg; sprinkle with raisins and breadcrumbs. Dot crumbs with butter.

Bake at 375°F for 20 minutes or until top is lightly browned.

Makes 4 servings.

MICROWAVE APPLE CRISP - VERSION 4

5-6 cooking apples, peeled and sliced
1/2 cup all-purpose flour
1/2 cup rolled oats (quick cooking)
3/4 cup brown sugar, firmly packed
1 tsp cinnamon
1/3 cup butter or margarine

Place apples in an 8"x 8" **microwavable** baking dish.

Combine flour, rolled oats, brown sugar and cinnamon. Cut in butter or margarine. Sprinkle over apples.

Cook, uncovered on high for 12 minutes in microwave oven or until apples are tender.

For a more crunchy and brown topping, place under the broiler for a few minutes.

Serves 4.

APPLE CRUNCH

1 1/2 lb tart apples
1 tbsp soft light brown sugar
1 tsp cinnamon
2 tbsp cold water

TOPPING

1 cup rolled oats
1/4 cup soft light brown sugar
1/4 cup whole wheat flour
salt, to taste
3 tbsp melted margarine

Preheat oven to 375°F. Grease a shallow 2-quart heatproof dish (this dessert can be served directly from the dish so select an attractive one if this is your choice).

Peel, quarter and core the apples, then thinly slice.

Mix the sugar with the cinnamon.

Layer the apple slices in the dish, sprinkling the spiced sugar mixture between the layers. Sprinkle the water over the apples.

To make the topping, mix the oats, sugar, flour and salt in a bowl. Stir in the melted margarine with a knife until thoroughly mixed.

Sprinkle the topping evenly over the apples. Bake for 50-60 minutes, until the apples are tender and the topping is crisp and browned. Serve hot or warm, straight from the dish.

Continued...

VARIATION:

Use all-purpose flour instead of whole wheat flour.

Halved and pitted plums can replace the apples, but they will need an extra tbsp of sugar.

A mixture of apples and blackberries could be used.

SERVING TIP:

Serve warm with vanilla ice cream, chilled sour cream or natural yogurt.

APPLE GRASMERE

(A French variation of Apple Crisp)

3 lb tart apples,
peeled, quartered, cored and sliced
3/4 cup white sugar
1/2 cup water

TOPPING:

1 1/2 cups all-purpose flour
1/2 tsp baking soda
1 tsp cream of tartar
2 tsp ground ginger
2/3 cups rolled oats (quick cooking)
1/2 cup soft dark brown sugar
3/4 cup margarine

Put the apples into a large, heavy-bottomed saucepan with the sugar and water. Cover and cook gently for 10-15 minutes, until reduced to a soft puree. Set aside to cool for about 30 minutes.

Meanwhile, preheat the oven to 350°F. Lightly grease a 1 1/4 quart heat-proof dish.

To make the topping, sift the flour with the baking soda, cream of tartar and ginger. Stir in the oats and brown sugar. Add margarine and rub in with fingertips until the mixture resembles fine bread crumbs.

Continued...

Spoon the cooled apple puree into the prepared dish, then top with the oat mixture, spreading it evenly on the apples.

Bake for about 30 minutes. Serve hot or cold.

SERVING IDEAS:

Top with lightly sweetened whipped cream.

Apple Grasmere is usually served chilled; the topping becomes crisp as it cools, making a mouth-watering contrast to the soft apple puree underneath.

SECTION L

CAKES

APPLE FILLING FOR LAYERED CAKES

2-3 cooking apples
1/4 cup fine white sugar
2 tbsp water
grated rind of 1 lemon
2-3 drops lemon juice
finely sieved cake crumbs
few drops food colouring
(your choice of colour)

Peel the apples and cut into quarters.

In a small saucepan, dissolve the sugar in the water.

Cool the syrup, put in the apple quarters, cover and stew gently until softened. Beat and drain off any liquid, then process through a nylon sieve*.

Add the lemon rind, juice, and enough cake crumbs to give a firm mixture. Colour pale pink, green or yellow with a few drops of food colouring.

Use as a filling for layered cakes.

* Old pantyhose (washed & bleached) make an excellent fine sieve

APPLE CAKE

2 cups all-purpose flour
2 tsp baking powder
1/2 tsp ground allspice
1/4 tsp ground nutmeg (optional)
1/2 cup margarine or butter, softened
3/4 cup light, soft brown sugar, packed
2 eggs, beaten
1/3 cup golden raisins
2 1/2 cups diced apples
2 tbsp raw sugar (or brown sugar)
shortening, for greasing

Preheat oven to 350°F. Line a deep 8" springform pan with aluminum foil and grease with shortening.

Sift the flour into a bowl. Sift in the baking powder, allspice and nutmeg. Mix well.

Using an electric mixer, beat the margarine and the brown sugar together until pale and fluffy. Add the eggs, a little at a time, beating thoroughly after each addition. If the mixture begins to curdle, add 1 tablespoon flour mixture with the next addition of egg.

Using a large metal spoon, fold dry flour mixture into wet egg mixture. Add the golden raisins and two-thirds of the diced apples. Turn into the prepared pan and level the surface.

Scatter the remaining apples evenly over the surface, then sprinkle over the raw sugar.

Bake the cake for about $1\frac{1}{2}$ hours, until the top is firm at the centre. Cover with waxed paper after 1 hour to prevent scorching.

Let the cake cool for 10 minutes, then remove from pan and peel off the foil. Cool completely on a wire rack.

APPLE UPSIDE-DOWN CAKE - VARIATION 1

Topping:

3 large baking apples (about 1 lb)
2 tbsp lemon juice
1/2 cup water
1/3 cup butter or margarine
3/4 cup firmly packed, light brown sugar
1/8 tsp cinnamon
2 tsp finely grated lemon peel
10 candied cherries

Cake batter:

1 3/4 cups all-purpose, or cake flour
1 tsp baking powder
1/2 tsp salt
3 egg yolks
1/2 cup granulated white sugar
1/3 cup orange juice
2 tbsp lemon juice
3 egg whites
1/2 cup sugar

Preheat oven to 350°F.

Sweetened whipped cream, optional.

For topping, peel, core and slice apples into ten 1/2" thick rings. Combine lemon juice with water and dip apple rings in the water to prevent browning.

Melt butter in a heavy 10" oven-safe pan (2" deep). Blend in brown sugar, salt, cinnamon, and lemon peel. Arrange apple rings in syrup, placing cherries in centre of each ring.

For cake batter, mix the flour with baking powder and salt; set aside.

Beat egg yolks until thick and lemon coloured. Gradually add 1/2 cup sugar and orange juice, beating thoroughly. Sift dry ingredients about one-fourth at a time over egg yolk mixture and gently fold until just blended after each addition. Set batter aside.

Beat egg whites until frothy. Gradually add 1/2 cup sugar, continuing to beat until stiff peaks are formed.

Gently fold batter into egg white mixture until just blended. Turn batter into pan over apple rings, spreading evenly.

Bake for 40-50 minutes, or until cake springs back when lightly touched.

Using a spatula, loosen cake from sides of pan and immediately turn over onto a serving plate. Allow pan to remain over cake a few seconds so syrup will drain onto cake. Remove pan.

Serve cake warm, topping each wedge with a spoonful of sweetened whipped cream, if desired.

APPLE UPSIDE-DOWN CAKE - VARIATION 2

1 cup flour
1/4 cup margarine
1/2 cup white sugar
1 beaten egg
1/2 cup milk
2 tsp baking powder
1/2 tsp vanilla
1/4 tsp salt

Sauce:

1 cup brown sugar
1 tbsp butter
1 tbsp flour
1/2 tsp vanilla
1 1/2 cup water

Preheat oven to 350°F.

Cream margarine and sugar. Stir in beaten egg.

Combine flour and baking powder. Alternately stir flour mixture, milk and vanilla into margarine mixture.

Chop 4 apples. Spread apples into 9" square cake pan. Pour batter over apples. Boil sauce for 10 minutes and pour sauce over batter.

Bake 30 minutes at 350°F. Serve with whipped cream.

APPLE JUICE CAKE

1 3/4 cups all-purpose flour
2 tsp baking powder
1/2 tsp salt
1/4 tsp baking soda
1/2 tsp cinnamon
1/4 tsp nutmeg
1/2 cup shortening
1 1/2 cups brown sugar (lightly packed)
2 eggs
1/2 cup milk
1/2 cup apple juice
1/2 cup chopped nuts

Preheat oven to 350°F. Grease two 8" round layer cake pans; line bottoms with wax paper OR dust lightly with flour.

Mix together first 6 ingredients (dry).

In large bowl, cream shortening and beat in brown sugar. Blend in the eggs, one at a time, then beat until light and fluffy.

Dry ingredients, as well as milk and apple juice will be added **alternately**, a little at a time, to wet mixture.

Fold in chopped nuts.

Divide mixture evenly into the two prepared pans and bake for 30-35 minutes or until cake springs back when lightly touched. Cool 5 minutes before removing from pans.

APPLESAUCE CAKE

2 1/2 cups all-purpose flour
2 cups granulated white sugar
1 1/2 tsp baking soda
1 1/2 tsp salt
1/4 tsp baking powder
3/4 tsp cinnamon
1/2 tsp cloves
1/2 tsp allspice
1 1/2 cups canned applesauce
1/2 cup water
1/2 cup shortening
2 eggs
1 cup raisins
1/2 cup finely chopped walnuts

Preheat oven to 350°F. Grease and flour baking pan, 13"x 9"x 2" or two 8" round layer pans.

Measure all ingredients into large mixer bowl. Blend 1/2 minute on low speed, scraping bowl constantly. Beat 3 minutes high speed, scraping bowl occasionally. Pour into pan(s).

Bake: oblong pan 60 to 65 minutes
layers 50 to 55 minutes

or until wooden pick inserted in centre comes out clean.

Cool.

Frost cake if desired.

SPICY MICROWAVE APPLESAUCE CAKE

1/2 cup shortening
2 cups granulated white sugar
2 eggs
2 1/2 cups all-purpose flour
1 1/2 tsp baking soda
1 1/2 tsp salt
1 tsp cinnamon
1/4 tsp baking powder
1/2 tsp cloves
1/4 tsp nutmeg
1 cup raisins
1/2 cup chopped walnuts
1 1/2 cups applesauce
1/2 cup water
1 tsp vanilla

MIXTURE A: Cream together shortening and sugar; beat in eggs.

MIXTURE B: Mix flour, soda, salt, baking powder, cinnamon, cloves, nutmeg, raisins and nuts.

Add flour Mixture B to shortening Mixture A; stir in applesauce, vanilla and water.

Line two 8" microwavable cake dishes with waxed paper. Pour half the batter into each prepared pan.

COOK ONE AT A TIME. Cook 6 1/2 to 7 minutes on high or until cake springs back when lightly touched. Let cake stand 5 minutes before turning on to cake rack.

EGGLESS APPLESAUCE CAKE

1/4 cup butter or margarine
1/3 cup granulated white sugar
1/4 tsp vanilla
1 cup all-purpose flour
3/4 tsp baking powder
1/2 tsp baking soda
5/8 cup unsweetened applesauce

Coconut Topping:

1/2 cup brown sugar
1 tsp butter
3 tbsp milk
1 cup coconut

Preheat oven to 350°F. Grease an 8" cake pan.

Cream butter and add vanilla; gradually add sugar. Mix dry ingredients. Add to first mixture alternately with applesauce, beginning and ending with dry ingredients. Stir gently and quickly until batter is well blended.

Spread carefully into prepared pan. Bake at 350°F for 35-40 minutes.

Allow cake to set 15 minutes before removing from pan.

Ice with coconut topping.

APPLE ALMOND CAKE

1/2 cup butter or margarine
2/3 cup icing sugar
2 eggs
1 cup all-purpose flour
1 tsp baking powder
1/3 cup milk
1 apple, grated
1/4 cup slivered almonds

Preheat oven to 350°F. Grease a deep 8" round cake pan.

Cream butter and sugar in small bowl until light and fluffy; beat in eggs, one at a time, until well mixed.

Transfer mixture to large bowl. Add half the flour, half the baking powder. Mix. Add half the milk; mix. Add remaining flour, baking powder and milk. Stir until smooth.

Spread into prepared pan. Sprinkle with apple and almonds.

Bake 45 minutes.

Cool on a wire rack - allow to cool 5 minutes before removing from pan.

MOIST APPLE AND DATE CAKE

2 apples, finely chopped
(Granny Smith are best)
1 cup chopped dates
1/2 tsp baking soda
1 cup boiling water
1 cup butter
1 cup fine white sugar
1 egg
2 cups all-purpose flour

MIXTURE A: combine chopped apples, dates, baking soda and boiling water in bowl; cover; cool.

Preheat oven to 325°F. Grease a 9" square cake pan.

MIXTURE B: Cream butter and sugar in small bowl until light and fluffy; beat in egg. Transfer mixture to a large bowl. Add flour and apple Mixture A.

Pour into prepared pan.

Bake 1 1/4 hours. Cool. Let stand for 5 minutes before turning onto wire rack to cool.

HAZELNUT APPLE CAKE

1 cup butter or margarine
3/4 cup fine white sugar
3 eggs
1/2 cup all-purpose flour
1/2 tsp baking powder
2 tbsp cocoa
1 3/4 cups roasted hazelnuts, ground fine
1 apple, grated
1/4 cup roasted hazelnuts, coarsely chopped

Preheat oven to 350°F. Grease a deep 8" round cake pan.

MIXTURE A: Cream butter and sugar in small bowl until light and fluffy. Beat in eggs one at a time until well mixed. Transfer to a large bowl.

MIXTURE B: Combine flour, baking powder and cocoa.

Add flour Mixture B to egg Mixture A. Fold in 1 3/4 cups hazelnuts and grated apple.

Spread into greased pan and bake 55 minutes. Allow to cool 5 minutes before turning on to wire rack to cool.

Spread with Lemon Icing (next page) and decorate with 1/4 cup chopped hazelnuts.

Continued...

LEMON ICING:

1/3 cup butter or margarine
1 cup icing sugar
1 tbsp lemon juice (approx.)

Beat butter in small bowl until light and fluffy. Gradually add icing sugar and then enough lemon juice to give a spreadable consistency and delicate lemon flavour.

APPLE/BUTTER CAKE

2/3 cup butter or margarine
1 tsp vanilla extract
3/4 cup fine white sugar
2 eggs
1 1/2 cups all-purpose flour
1 tsp baking powder
1/2 cup milk
1 cup chopped fresh apple
OR
1/2 cup canned apple pie filling

Preheat oven to 350°F. Grease 9"x 13"x 2" pan.

In a small bowl, cream butter with vanilla and sugar until light and fluffy; beat in eggs one at a time.

Transfer to large bowl; stir in half the flour and baking powder, then half the milk. Mix well.

Add remaining flour, baking powder and milk.

Spread 2/3 of the mixture into the greased pan. Spread an even layer of apples on batter. Cover with remaining cake mixture.

Bake 35 minutes.

Allow to cool 10 minutes before turning on wire rack to cool OR cool and serve in pan.

APPLE CHOCOLATE CAKE

(Prepared in Food Processor)

1 cup butter or margarine
1 1/4 cups fine white sugar
3 eggs
1/3 cup cocoa
1/4 tsp baking soda
1/3 cup water
2 cups all-purpose flour
2 tsp baking powder
2 apples, peeled, quartered
(Granny Smith preferred)

Preheat oven to 350°F. Grease 9"x 13"x 2" pan.

Combine butter, sugar, eggs, cocoa, water and apple in Food Processor. Mix well. Add flour, baking soda, baking powder and blend until mixture is smooth.

Pour into greased pan. Bake 1 hour. Allow to cool 5 minutes before turning on to wire rack to cool OR cool and serve in pan. Spread with:

CHOCOLATE ICING:

1 cup icing sugar
1 tbsp cocoa
1 tsp soft butter or margarine
1 tbsp milk (approx.)

Combine icing sugar and cocoa into small heat-proof bowl; stir in butter and enough milk to make a stiff paste. Stir over hot water until icing is spreadable.

SPICY APPLE AND CURRANT YOGURT CAKE

2/3 cup butter or margarine
2 tsp grated lemon rind
3/4 cup fine white sugar
2 eggs
1 cup plain yogurt
1 cup unsweetened apple pie filling
3/4 cups currants
2 cups all-purpose flour
1 tsp baking powder
1/2 tsp baking soda
2 tsp allspice

Preheat oven to 350°F. Grease a 9" square pan.

MIXTURE A: Beat butter, rind and sugar in small bowl until light and fluffy. Beat in eggs, one at a time, and continue beating until well mixed. Stir in yogurt, apple and currants.

MIXTURE B: Mix flour, baking powder, baking soda and allspice.

MIXTURE C: Pour Mixture B into Mixture A.

Spread into greased pan and bake for about 55 minutes.

Let stand 5 minutes before turning on to wire rack to cool. Dust with sifted icing sugar before serving.

CARAMEL APPLE CAKE

1 1/4 cups all-purpose flour
1 1/2 tsp ground cinnamon
1/2 tsp baking powder
1 1/2 cups brown sugar, firmly packed
1 tsp vanilla
1/3 cup butter or margarine
3 eggs
2 apples, grated
1 cup walnuts, chopped
1/2 cup raisins

Preheat oven to 350°F. Grease a deep 8" square cake pan.

Mix together the sugar, vanilla, butter and eggs in a large bowl.

In another bowl, combine dry ingredients and add to butter mixture. Blend until ingredients are combined, then beat for about 3 minutes or until mixture is changed in colour and is smooth.

Stir in apples, nuts and raisins.

Spread into prepared pan and bake for about 50 minutes.

Let stand 5 minutes before turning on to wire rack to cool.

OLD FASHIONED APPLE LOAF

1 cup all-purpose flour
1 cup whole wheat flour
1 tsp baking powder
1 tsp baking soda
1/2 tsp salt
1/4 tsp allspice
1/8 tsp cloves
1/4 cup butter
3/4 cup brown sugar
1 egg
3/4 cup buttermilk
3 apples
1/2 cup chopped walnuts

Preheat oven to 350°F. Grease an 8 1/2"x 4 1/2"x 2 1/2" loaf pan.

MIXTURE A: Combine all-purpose flour, whole wheat flour, baking powder, baking soda, salt, allspice and cloves.

MIXTURE B: Cream butter and brown sugar in large bowl. Add egg and buttermilk and mix well.

Peel, core and shred apples (should measure about 1 1/2 cups). Add to creamed Mixture B. Stir in walnuts. Stir flour Mixture A into creamed Mixture B. Pour into prepared pan.

Bake for 1 hour.

GLAZED APPLE CAKE

(Apple Pan Cake Brulee)

4 cups peeled and diced apples (approx. 4 medium)
1/2 cup brown sugar
1/4 cup chopped walnuts
1 cup all-purpose flour
1 tsp baking powder
3 eggs
1 cup light cream
1 1/2 tsp vanilla extract
1/4 tsp salt

Preheat oven to 375°F. Grease a 10" ovenproof pan or shallow baking dish.

Toss apples with 1/4 cup of brown sugar and walnuts; spoon into prepared pan.

In small bowl, combine flour and baking powder.

With mixer, blend eggs, cream, vanilla and salt. On low speed, slowly add flour mixture; mix 30 seconds. Pour over apples.

Bake for 40 minutes or until centre is done. Sprinkle remaining brown sugar over top and broil 8 inches from heat until lightly caramelized, about 2 minutes. Serve warm with vanilla-flavoured whipped cream.

Makes 8 servings.

APPLE CHEESECAKE SUPREME

1 cup all-purpose flour
1/4 cup brown sugar (firmly packed)
1/2 cup butter or margarine
1 pkg (8 oz) cream cheese, softened
1/4 cup + 2 tbsp granulated white sugar
1 tsp grated lemon rind
1 egg
6 medium apples, peeled and thinly sliced
1 tbsp lemon juice
1/4 cup apple jelly

Preheat oven to 400°F.

Combine flour and brown sugar; cut in butter until mixture is crumbly. Press evenly over bottom, and 1" up the sides of a 9" springform pan. Bake at 400°F for 10 minutes. Remove from oven and reduce temperature to 350°F.

Beat cream cheese, 1/2 cup granulated white sugar and lemon rind until fluffy. Beat in egg. Pour into baked crust.

Combine apples, remaining sugar and lemon juice. Spoon evenly over cheese layer; press down gently. Bake for about 35 minutes.

Melt apple jelly in small saucepan over low heat. Brush over surface of apples. Cool, then chill before serving.

Makes 10-12 servings.

APPLE BAVARIAN TORTE

1/2 cup butter or margarine
1/3 cup granulated white sugar
1/4 tsp vanilla
1 cup all-purpose flour
1 pkg (8 oz) cream cheese, softened,
    at room temperature
1/4 cup granulated white sugar
1 egg
1/2 tsp vanilla
4 cups apples, peeled and sliced
1/3 cup brown sugar, lightly packed
cinnamon to taste (approx. 1 tsp)
2 cups sliced almonds

Preheat oven to 450°F.

Cream margarine, 1/3 cup white sugar and vanilla. Add flour and spread in an 8" or 9" springform pan, uncooked.

Combine cheese with 1/4 cup white sugar; add egg and vanilla. Stir well until mixture is creamy and smooth. Pour on prepared crust.

Combine brown sugar and cinnamon with apples and spoon mixture over the cream cheese mixture. Sprinkle almonds to cover.

Bake at 450°F for 10 minutes, then lower to 400° for 25 minutes. Best served warm with sweetened whipped cream.

APPLE SPICE CAKE WITH MERINGUE

1/2 cup butter or shortening
1 tsp vanilla extract
2/3 cup firmly packed brown sugar
2 eggs
1 egg yolk
1 3/4 cups all-purpose flour
2 1/2 tsp baking powder
1/2 tsp salt
3/4 tsp baking soda
1/2 tsp cinnamon
1/8 tsp allspice
1/8 tsp nutmeg
3 tbsp milk
1/2 cup dairy sour cream
1 1/2 cups apple, peeled, chopped

MERINGUE TOPPING:

4 egg whites
1 cup granulated white sugar
1/8 tsp salt
1/2 cup chopped walnuts

Preheat oven to 325°F. Grease a 9" x 13" x 2" baking pan.

Cream butter with vanilla in large bowl. Add brown sugar and mix well. Add eggs and egg yolk; mix well.

Combine flour with baking powder, baking soda, cinnamon, salt, allspice, and nutmeg. Add dry ingredients to creamed mixture alternately with milk and sour cream, mixing well after each addition.

Continued

Stir in chopped apple; mix well. Spoon batter into prepared baking pan, spreading evenly with a spatula.

Beat egg whites until they hold soft peaks. Beating continuously, gradually add sugar and salt. Continue to beat 1 minute after sugar has been added.

Spoon the meringue over cake batter around edge. Using a spatula, gently spread meringue toward the centre, leaving a space of 1 1/2" in diameter in centre of cake. Sprinkle walnuts over meringue.

Bake at 325°F for 45 minutes. Set pan on a wire rack and allow cake to cool in pan.

APPLE AND APRICOT LOAF

1/2 cup chopped dried apples
1/2 cup chopped dried apricots
3/4 cup boiling water
1/2 cup butter or margarine
3/4 cup fine white sugar
2 eggs
1/3 cup shredded coconut
1/3 cup golden corn syrup
2 cups all-purpose flour
1 tsp baking powder
1/2 tsp baking soda
1/4 cup milk

MIXTURE A: Combine apples, apricots and boiling water in bowl, cool to room temperature.

Grease a 5" x 8" loaf pan, line base and sides with waxed paper. Preheat oven to 325°F.

MIXTURE B: Cream butter and sugar in small bowl with electric mixer. Beat in eggs, one at a time, until well-mixed. Transfer to a large bowl. Stir in undrained apple/apricot mixture and golden corn syrup.

MIXTURE C: Combine dry ingredients, flour, baking powder, baking soda.

MIXTURE D: In wet Mixture B, stir in half of dry Mixture C; add half the milk. Add remaining dry Mixture C and remaining milk.

Pour into prepared pan. Bake for about 1 1/4 hours. Stand 5 minutes before turning on to wire rack to cool.

SPRINGFORM APPLE CAKE

1 cup butter or margarine
2 tsp grated lemon rind
2/3 cup fine white sugar
3 eggs
1 1/2 cups all-purpose flour
1 tsp baking powder
1/2 tsp baking soda
1/3 cup milk
2 apples, peeled, cored and quartered
1 tsp gelatine
2 tbsp water
2 tbsp strained apricot jam

Grease an 8" springform pan. Preheat oven to 350°F.

MIXTURE A: Cream butter, rind and sugar in small bowl with electric mixer until light and fluffy. Beat in eggs one at a time and continue beating until well mixed. Transfer mixture to a large bowl.

MIXTURE B: Mix all dry ingredients.

MIXTURE C: Pour dry ingredients (Mixture B) into wet (Mixture A). Add milk.

Spread into prepared pan.

Make lengthways cuts into rounded sides of apple quarters, cutting about 3/4 of the way through. Arrange apple quarters, rounded side up, around edge of cake. Bake for about 1 hour.

Sprinkle gelatine over 2 tbsp water; dissolve over hot water and add jam. Spread half jam mixture over hot cake, cool cake in pan.

Remove from pan. Warm remaining jam mixture and brush over cooled cake.

APPLE GATEAU

2 1/2 lb tart apples, peeled, cored and sliced
6 cloves
finely peeled rind of 1 lemon
1/2 cup fine white sugar
(increase or decrease amount to taste)
2 tbsp water
1/2 cup butter or margarine
4 cups graham cracker crumbs
1 tsp cinnamon

TO DECORATE:

3/4 cup heavy cream
1 oz (1 square) semi-sweet chocolate,
coarsely grated
6 candied cherries

Grease a deep 8" round springform cake pan.

Put apples, cloves, lemon rind, sugar and water into a saucepan. Cook, uncovered, over very low heat for about 25 minutes, stirring frequently, until the apples are disintegrating.

Meanwhile, melt the butter in a separate heavy-bottomed saucepan over low heat. Remove from the heat and gradually stir in crumbs, then stir in the cinnamon.

Remove the cooked apples from the heat. Discard the cloves and lemon rind, then beat vigorously with a wooden spoon to make a very thick, chunky pulp.

Spoon one-third of the crumb mixture into the prepared pan and press firmly over the bottom. Spread half the apples over the crumbs. Spoon half the remaining crumbs over the apples and press down lightly. Spread with the rest of the apples, then cover with a layer of the remaining crumbs.

Cover the pan with plastic wrap and refrigerate for at least 12 hours (and up to 48 hours).

To serve, remove the sides of the pan, then transfer the gateau (still on pan bottom) to a cake plate. Whip the cream until it forms soft peaks and spread over top of gateau. Sprinkle with the coarsely grated chocolate.

Cut 5 cherries in half and place around the top edge of the gateau. Using a long sharp knife, carefully cut gateau into 10 slices. Place the remaining whole cherry in the centre.

Serve at once or return to the refrigerator for up to 2 hours.

SECTION M

MUFFINS

The general practice when making muffins is to mix the dry ingredients together in one bowl then mix the wet ingredients together in another; stir just until mixed and cook immediately.

Do not overmix; this will make your muffins heavy.

Add nuts and raisins when making apple muffins; both are great with apples, and they add flavour, variety and additional nutrition.

For extra-healthy muffins, reduce amount of flour by 1/3 cup and add 1/3 cup of wheat germ.

Always out of milk? Keep a supply of powdered skim milk on hand and use it when baking. Simply add 1/3 cup skim milk powder to your dry ingredients and substitute the appropriate amount of water for the specified amount of milk.

APPLESAUCE OATMEAL MUFFINS

1 cup all-purpose flour
3 tsp baking powder
1/2 tsp cinnamon
1/2 tsp salt
1/4 tsp nutmeg
3/4 cup rolled oats
1/4 cup brown sugar (lightly packed)
1 egg
1/4 cup vegetable oil
1/3 cup milk
1/3 cup sweetened applesauce

Preheat oven to 400° F. Grease (or add paper liners to) 12 muffin cups.

MIXTURE A: Measure dry ingredients into a large mixing bowl. Stir with a fork until well-blended.

MIXTURE B: Whisk or beat together egg, oil and milk. Stir in applesauce. Pour into dry ingredients (Mixture A) and stir just until all ingredients are moist. **DO NOT OVERMIX**

Fill prepared muffin cups 2/3 full. Bake in preheated oven for 15 minutes.

Preparation time: 10 minutes
Baking time: 15 minutes

About 129 calories per muffin

APPLESAUCE BRAN MUFFINS

1 cup All Bran cereal
1 cup buttermilk*
1 1/4 cup smooth, sweetened applesauce
1/4 cup molasses
1/4 cup cooking oil
1 egg
1 tsp vanilla
1 cup all-purpose flour
1/3 cup brown sugar, lightly packed
1 tsp salt
1 tsp baking soda

* if you do not have buttermilk, measure 1 tbsp lemon juice or vinegar into a 1 cup measure, fill with milk and let stand 5 minutes.

Preheat oven to 375°F. Grease (or line with paper) 12 large or 18 small muffin cups.

MIXTURE A: Into a large bowl measure the bran, buttermilk, applesauce, molasses, oil, egg and vanilla. Give a good stir and let stand 5 minutes.

MIXTURE B: Measure dry ingredients into another bowl.

Stir dry Mixture B into wet Mixture A until barely blended. Spoon batter into prepared muffin cups to 3/4 full.

Bake in preheated oven for 20 minutes for large muffins, 18 minutes for small.

APPLE CINNAMON MUFFINS

1 large apple, peeled & diced
1 tsp lemon juice
1 1/2 tsp cinnamon
pinch of nutmeg
2 1/2 cups all-purpose flour
4 tsp baking powder
1/3 cup granulated white sugar
1/3 cup brown sugar, lightly packed
2 eggs
1 cup milk
1/2 cup butter or margarine, melted

Preheat oven to 400°F. Grease (or line with paper) 12 muffin cups.

MIXTURE A: Combine diced apple with lemon juice, cinnamon and nutmeg. Set aside.

MIXTURE B: Combine flour, baking powder, brown sugar, and white sugar in a large bowl. Mix well.

MIXTURE C: Beat eggs with milk and melted butter.

Pour wet Mixture C over dry Mixture B. Combine only until blended. Stir in apple Mixture A.

Spoon muffin mixture into prepared muffins tins. Bake in preheated oven for 25 minutes.

Preparation Time: 15 minutes
Baking Time: 25 minutes

POPULAR APPLE MUFFINS

1 cup grated apple
1 egg
1/2 cup milk
1/4 cup salad oil
1 1/2 cups all-purpose flour
1/2 cup granulated white sugar
2 tsp baking powder
1/2 tsp salt
1/2 tsp cinnamon

NUT CRUNCH TOPPING:

Mix 1/3 cup brown sugar (packed), 1/3 cup broken nuts and 1/2 tsp cinnamon.

Preheat oven to 400°F. Grease (or line with paper) bottoms of 12 medium muffin cups (2 3/4 inches in diameter).

MIXTURE A: Beat egg; stir in milk, oil and grated apple.

MIXTURE B: Mix dry ingredients.

Pour dry ingredients (Mixture B) into wet (Mixture A), mix until just moistened. Batter should be lumpy.

Fill muffin cups 2/3 full. Sprinkle tops with Nut Crunch Topping. Bake 20 to 25 minutes or until golden brown. Immediately remove from pan.

APPLESAUCE MUFFINS WITH PRUNES

3/4 cup all-purpose flour
1/2 tsp cinnamon
1/2 tsp salt
1/4 tsp nutmeg
1 tbsp baking powder
1 1/4 cup rolled oats
3/4 cup chopped prunes
1/2 cup brown sugar, lightly packed
1/2 cup vegetable oil
1 egg
1 cup applesauce

Preheat oven to 400°F. Grease (or line with paper) 12 muffin cups.

MIXTURE A: Mix flour, cinnamon, salt, nutmeg and baking powder together in large bowl. Mix in rolled oats, chopped prunes and brown sugar. Mix well.

MIXTURE B: Beat oil and egg together; mix in applesauce.

MIXTURE C: Pour wet Mixture B into dry Mixture A. Stir to blend - DO NOT OVERMIX!

Fill muffin cups and bake 20 minutes.

APPLESAUCE MUFFINS WITH WHOLE WHEAT FLOUR

1 2/3 cups whole wheat flour
1/3 cup wheat germ
1/2 cup brown sugar
2 tsp baking powder
1/4 tsp salt
1/3 cup vegetable oil
1/3 cup milk
2 eggs
2/3 cup applesauce

Preheat oven to 350°F. Grease (or line with paper) 12 muffin cups.

MIXTURE A: Mix all dry ingredients together in large bowl.

MIXTURE B: In small bowl, mix all wet ingredients.

MIXTURE C: Pour wet Mixture B into dry Mixture A. Stir to blend - DO NOT OVERMIX!

Fill muffin cups and bake 20-25 minutes.

EASY, HEALTHY APPLE MUFFINS
(Mixed in blender)

1/3 cup vegetable oil
3/4 cup brown sugar, lightly packed
1 egg
2/3 cup milk
2 medium apples, cored but not peeled
(cut in quarters or eighths)
1 1/4 cups all-purpose flour
1/2 cup whole wheat flour
1/4 cup wheat germ
3/4 tsp baking soda
1/2 tsp salt
2 tsp baking powder
1/4 tsp cinnamon

TOPPING MIXTURE

1 tsp cinnamon
1 1/2 tbsp granulated white sugar

Preheat oven to 375°F. Grease (or line with paper) 12 medium muffin cups.

MIXTURE A: IN BLENDER, put milk, egg, oil, sugar, nuts and apple. Blend well.

MIXTURE B: In large bowl, combine all dry ingredients.

MIXTURE C: Pour blender Mixture A into dry Mixture B and stir only until mixed.

Fill muffin cups; sprinkle with sugar/cinnamon topping mixture and bake for 20 minutes.

APPLE MUFFINS WITH CHEDDAR CHEESE (and coffee!)

3 medium apples,
peeled and sliced into 1/4" slices
1 cup granulated white sugar
1 1/2 tbsp cinnamon
1/4 cup chopped walnuts
1/2 cup butter or margarine
2 eggs
1 1/2 cups all-purpose flour
1 tsp baking soda
1 tsp baking powder
1/2 tsp salt
1/4 tsp almond extract
1 cup grated old or medium cheddar cheese
1/4 cup "Camp" coffee (concentrated liquid)
or 1/4 cup water with 3 tsp powdered instant coffee

Preheat oven to 375°F. Grease (or line with paper) 18 medium muffin cups.

Mix 1/2 cup white sugar and 1 tbsp cinnamon in small bowl. This leaves 1/2 cup white sugar and 1/2 tbsp cinnamon to be added to dry ingredients.

Select 18 apple slices and sprinkle with sugar/ cinnamon mixture; toss. Set aside apples. Add chopped walnuts to bowl of remaining sugar/ cinnamon mixture (topping).

In large bowl, cream butter with remaining 1/2 cup of white sugar and eggs.

Continued...

In second bowl, mix all dry ingredients together. Stir dry ingredients into wet ingredients and mix just enough to blend. Stir in chopped apple, cheese and coffee.

Place some of mixture in each muffin cup (about 1/4 full). Press 1 slice of sugared apple into each cup. Add remainder of batter to fill cups. Sprinkle with sugar/cinnamon/nut mixture and bake for 20-25 minutes.

CHUNKY WHOLE WHEAT APPLE MUFFINS

1/4 cup vegetable oil
3/4 cup brown sugar, lightly packed
1 egg
1 tbsp sour cream or yogurt
1 1/2 cups chopped apple (peeled)
1/2 cup raisins*
1 cup whole wheat flour
3/4 tsp baking soda
3/4 tsp salt
1 tsp baking powder
1/4 tsp cinnamon
1/4 tsp nutmeg

TOPPING MIXTURE

1 tsp cinnamon
1 1/2 tbsp white sugar

Preheat oven to 375°F. Grease (or line with paper) 12 medium muffin cups.

* Soak raisins in hot water for several minutes before draining and using in recipe; this will make them plump and juicy.

MIXTURE A: Using large bowl, beat oil, sugar, egg and cream (or yogurt). Stir in apple and raisins (drained).

MIXTURE B: Mix all dry ingredients together.

Continued...

MIXTURE C: Pour dry Mixture B into wet Mixture A. Stir to just blend ingredients.

Fill muffin cups; sprinkle with sugar/cinnamon topping mixture and bake for 20 minutes.

SECTION N

CREPES AND PANCAKES

DESSERT CREPES

Dessert crepes should be as thin and delicate as possible. The lightness of the crepe can be attributed to the use of milk diluted with water. ***The batter for dessert crepes must rest at least two hours before using, however they may be made several hours before serving time.*** Pile crepes in a dish; then cover with waxed paper and a plate to keep them from drying out until ready to use.

METHOD FOR COOKING CREPES

If using a crepe pan, follow the cooking directions provided with it.

If you do not have a crepe pan, lightly brush an iron or non-stick fry pan with oil. Set over moderately high heat until the pan is just beginning to smoke.

Immediately remove from heat and, holding the handle of the pan in one hand, pour with the other hand a scant 1/4 cup of batter into the middle of the pan. Quickly tilt the pan in all directions to run the batter all over the bottom of the pan in a thin film (pour any batter that does not adhere to the pan back into your bowl; judge the amount for your next crepe accordingly). The whole operation takes only 2 or 3 seconds.

Continued...

Return the pan to heat for 60-80 seconds. Then jerk and toss pan sharply back and forth and up and down to loosen the crepe. Lift its edges with a spatula and if the under side is a nice light brown, the crepe is ready for turning.

Turn the crepe by using 2 spatulas; or grasp the edges nearest you in your fingers and sweep it up toward you and over again into the pan in a reverse circle; or toss it over by a flip of the pan.

Brown lightly for about 1/2 minute on second side; this side is rarely more than a spotty brown and is always kept on the underneath or "non-public" side of the crepe.

Slide crepe onto a plate and repeat the process. Once you have mastered the skill, you can have two fry pans going at once and complete 24 crepes in less than half and hour.

LIGHT CREPES

3/4 cup milk
3/4 cup cold water
3 egg yolks
1 tbsp granulated white sugar
3 tbsp brandy, orange liqueur, or rum
1 1/2 cups all-purpose flour
5 tbsp melted butter or margarine

Place all ingredients in electric blender jar in the order in which they are listed. Cover and blend at top speed for 1 minute. If bits of flour adhere to sides of jar dislodge with a rubber scraper and blend 3 seconds more. Cover and refrigerate for at least 2 hours or over night.

IF YOU DO NOT HAVE AN ELECTRIC BLENDER:

Gradually work the egg yolks into the flour with a wooden spoon, beat in the liquids by droplets, then strain the batter through a fine sieve.

Makes 10 to 12 crepes, 6 inches in diameter.

YEAST BATTER FOR STUFFED CREPES

Same ingredients as for Light Crepes
1 1/2 tsp fresh or dry yeast

Warm 1/4 cup of the milk to approximately body temperature and allow the yeast to dissolve in it. Add it to the rest of the ingredients in the blender and proceed with the recipe.

Cover the batter with a towel and let it stand at room temperature for about 2 hours, or until the yeast has worked and the batter looks bubbly on top. Use immediately, or the yeast will over-ferment.

RAISED BATTER - FOR STUFFED CREPES

Same ingredients as for Light Crepes
3 egg whites
pinch of salt

Beaten egg whites folded into the batter make the crepes pull slightly.

After the batter has rested for 2 hours, and just before you wish to make your crepes, beat the egg whites and salt until stiff. Fold half into the batter, fold in the other half, then make the crepes.

HAM AND APPLE STUFFED CREPES

2 apples, cored, peeled and diced
lemony cold water to cover apple
(2 tbsp lemon juice/1/2 cup cold water)
2 tbsp butter or margarine
1 red pepper, chopped
3 green onions, sliced
1/2 lb fresh mushrooms, cleaned and diced
2 cups cubed cooked ham
1 tbsp chopped fresh parsley
1/4 tsp marjoram
4 tbsp all-purpose flour
2 cups chicken stock, heated
1 1/2 cups grated Gruyere (or Old Cheddar) cheese
8 crepes
salt and pepper
dash of paprika
pinch of nutmeg
few crushed chilies
pinch of powdered cloves

Place chopped apples in small bowl filled with lemony cold water. Set aside.

Reserving 1 tsp butter; melt remainder in large fry pan over medium heat. Add red pepper, green onions and mushrooms; cook 3-4 minutes. Drain apples and add to pan. Mix in ham, cover and cook 6 minutes over low heat. Add parsley and all seasonings; mix well. Stir in flour until well mixed; cover and cook 3 minutes over low heat.

Continued...

Pour in chicken stock, adjust seasoning to suit your taste and bring to boil. Cook 5-6 minutes, uncovered over medium heat. Mix in half of cheese and cook 2 minutes.

Preheat oven to 400°F.

Lay crepes flat on cutting board. Using slotted spoon, divide filling onto crepes; fold each in half and then in half again to form triangle. Place in large baking dish, pour in remaining sauce and top with rest of cheese.

Dot with 1 tsp butter, season with pepper and bake 5 minutes.

GERMAN APPLE PANCAKES

BATTER:

8 large eggs
1 cup all-purpose flour
2 tbsp granulated white sugar
1 tsp baking powder
1/8 tsp salt
2 cups milk
1/4 cup butter or margarine, melted
2 tsp vanilla extract
1/4 tsp nutmeg

Beat egg; add remaining ingredients in order listed and beat with rotary beater until smooth. Set aside.

APPLE MIXTURE:

1/2 cup butter (unsalted preferred)
1 1/3 cups granulated white sugar
1 tsp cinnamon
1/4 tsp nutmeg
2 large, tart apples, peeled, sliced
(about 2 cups)

Preheat oven to 475°F.

Divide butter evenly and melt on top of stove in two 10-inch fry pans. Brush butter up sides of pan. Remove pans from heat.

Combine sugar, cinnamon, nutmeg and blend well. Sprinkle 1/3 cup sugar-spice mixture evenly over butter in each fry pan. Divide apple slices; layer evenly over spice layer.

Continued...

Sprinkle remaining sugar over apple layers in fry pans. Place fry pans over medium heat; cook until mixture bubbles. Pour half of the batter into each fry pan.

Place fry pans on racks in centre of 425°F oven. Bake 15 minutes; reduce heat to 375°F. Bake 10 minutes longer, or until brown and crisp.

Slide pancakes onto heated serving platter. Slice to serve hot. (Using a pizza cutter makes slicing easy).

Serves 4 to 6

FAVOURITE APPLE PANCAKES

1 egg
1/2 cup buttermilk *
1/2 cup applesauce
2 tbsp salad oil
1 cup all-purpose flour **
1 tbsp granulated white sugar
1 tbsp baking powder
1/2 tsp baking soda
1/2 tsp salt

* If you do not have buttermilk, refer to Section P - TIPS for alternative.

** you may substitute whole-wheat flour; if you do, then double the amount of both baking powder and baking soda.

Beat egg; add remaining ingredients in order listed and beat with rotary beater until smooth. Grease heated griddle if necessary. To test griddle, sprinkle with few drops of water. If bubbles skitter around, heat is just right.

Pour batter from tip of large spoon or from pitcher onto hot griddle. Turn pancakes as soon as they are puffed and full of bubbles but before bubbles break. Cook other side until golden brown.

Makes 10 4-inch pancakes.

CREPES WITH APPLES, FLAMBE

2 lbs crisp cooking or eating apples
1/2 cup + 2 tbsp granulated white sugar
(or more to taste)
2 tbsp whipping cream
1/4 tsp almond extract
2 tbsp + 1/2 cup Calvados (apple brandy),
cognac, or dark rum
10 to 12 cooked crepes
(refer to one of the recipes at beginning
of section - pages 187-190)
butter or margarine (to grease dish)
1/2 cup finely crushed almonds
2 tbsp slivered almonds
2 tbsp melted butter or margarine

Quarter, core and peel the apples. Chop them roughly (about 5 cups).

Cook in a covered pan over low heat for about 20 minutes, stirring occasionally, until apples are tender. Uncover, add 1/2 cup sugar, raise heat and boil, stirring, for 5 minutes or more. Applesauce should reduce and be thick enough to hold itself in a fairly solid mass in the spoon. Add more sugar while the apples are cooking to achieve the taste you want.

Add the cream, almond extract, and the 2 tbsp brandy to the applesauce.

At the bottom of a lightly buttered baking/serving dish, centre a crepe.

Spread a layer of apples over it and sprinkle with a scant tablespoon of crushed almonds. Continue with layers of crepe, apples, and almonds, ending with a crepe. This will look like a many-layered cake.

Sprinkle the slivered almonds over the last crepe; pour on the melted butter and sprinkle with 2 tbsp sugar.

About 30 minutes before serving, place in the upper third of a preheated, 375°F oven to heat through thoroughly. The sugar on top of the mound should almost begin to caramelize.

TO SERVE:

Warm 1/2 cup brandy in a small saucepan. Immediately before serving crepes, pour warmed brandy over the hot mound of crepes. Set liqueur aflame with a lighted match.

BE SURE TO AVERT YOUR FACE

Use extreme caution to prevent burns.

Present the blazing dessert. Spoon the flaming liqueur over the dessert until the fire subsides, then cut portions from the mound as from a cake.

VARIATIONS:

Crepes may also be rolled or folded instead of piled high.

Substitute crushed macaroons for almonds.

Continued...

Fresh fruits: let strawberries, raspberries, or sliced bananas stand in a bowl with a sprinkling of sugar and kirsch, orange liqueur, or cognac for an hour; use as filling in place of apples.

Jams, Preserves, and Jellies: make delicious desserts when the crepes are flamed with liqueur. Mix a little kirsch, cognac, or orange liqueur into red currant jelly, or raspberry, strawberry, apricot, or cherry jam or preserves; use as filling in place of apples.

CLAFOUTI

The **clafouti** is traditional French peasant cooking during the cherry season and a simple dessert to make: a pancake batter poured over fruit in a baking dish, then baked.

Traditional Cherry Clafouti

BATTER:

1 1/4 cups milk
1/3 cup granulated white sugar
3 eggs
1 tbsp vanilla extract
1/8 tsp salt
2/3 cup all-purpose flour

FILLING:

3 cups pitted black cherries
(fresh if available, otherwise canned Bing cherries, or frozen sweet cherries - thawed and drained)
1/3 cup granulated white sugar

Preheat oven to 350°F.

Place all batter ingredients in an electric blender jar (if you do not have a blender, refer to page 189 for direction).

Cover and blend at top speed for 1 minute.

Use a baking dish or pie plate that will hold 7-8 cups and can be used **both on the stove and in the oven.** Lightly butter the pan and pour a layer of batter 1/4 inch thick. Set over moderate heat for a minute or two until a film of batter has set in the bottom of the dish. Remove from heat.

Spread the cherries over the batter and sprinkle with sugar. Pour on the rest of the batter and smooth the surface with the back of a spoon.

Place in middle position of preheated oven and bake for about one hour. The clafouti is done when it has puffed and browned, and a knife plunged into its centre comes out clean.

Sprinkle top of clafouti with powdered sugar just before serving. Serve WARM. Note that the clafouti will sink down slightly as it cools.

VARIATIONS

Cherry Clafouti with Liqueur

Follow the above recipe but first let the cherries stand for 1 hour in a mixture of 1/4 cup kirsch or cognac and 1/3 cup of sugar. Then substitute this liquid for part of the milk called for in the batter; omit the sugar over the cherries near the end of the recipe.

Apple Clafouti

Follow the Traditional Cherry recipe with the following changes:

Substitute 1 1/4 lbs crisp eating or cooking apples for cherries; peel, core and slice lengthwise 1/4 inch thick (approx. 3 cups).

Saute to brown very lightly in 3-4 tbsp hot butter. Remove from heat. Mix 1/4 cup Calvados (apple brandy), cognac or dark rum with 1/8 tsp cinnamon and 1/3 cup sugar. Pour over apples, then let stand in the fry pan for 1/2 hour.

Substitute this liquid for part of the milk called for in the batter; omit the sugar over the apples near the end of the recipe.

Blueberry or Blackberry Clafouti

Follow the Traditional Cherry recipe with the following changes:

Substitute 3 cups of washed berries for cherries; increase flour for batter from 2/3 cup to 1 1/4 cups because berries are very juicy.

SECTION O

SALADS

APPLE BEEF SALAD

Use McIntosh or Red Delicious Apples for best results.

2 medium apples (cored, unpeeled, diced)
1 cup cooked cold roast beef
(thin strips 1 1/2 to 2" long)
1 small garlic clove, minced
4 green onions, finely sliced
1 cup celery, diced
1/4 cup parsley, minced
6 tbsp salad oil
3 tsp cider vinegar
1/2 tsp salt
1/4 tsp pepper

Toss all ingredients together. Cover and refrigerate until well chilled.

Makes 4 servings.

APPLE 'N CHEESE SLAW

4 cups finely shredded or chopped cabbage
(about 1/2 medium head)
2 cups tart apples, diced, unpeeled
(McIntosh, Granny Smith are good choices; refer to TIPS Section - pages 216-218 for other selections of tart apples)
1/2 cup blue cheese, crumbled
1/2 cup dairy sour cream
1/4 cup mayonnaise or salad dressing
1/2 tsp salt
paprika, a sprinkle to taste

Combine cabbage, apples and blue cheese in large salad bowl.

Blend remaining ingredients; pour over cabbage mixture and toss.

If desired, sprinkle with paprika.

Serves 6-8

APPLE AND CELERY SALAD

Dressing:

8 tbsp cooking oil
4 tbsp wine vinegar
2 tsp (level) Dijon mustard
1 tbsp chopped onion
1 tbsp chopped parsley
black pepper, freshly ground - to taste

Salad:

2 heads celery
3 oz walnuts, chopped
5 red eating apples, cored, cubed, but not peeled

Make the dressing by placing all ingredients into a screw-topped jar and shaking well. Chill for 30 minutes.

Trim the ends off the celery and split up into sticks. Wash and cut into thin "julienne" strips about 2 inches long.

Cut the walnuts in small pieces and place in a bowl with the celery.

Toss in the cubed apples.

Pour enough of the chilled dressing over to moisten all ingredients and then toss lightly.

Serves 4-6

WINTER FRUIT BOWL

1 can (16 oz) pitted dark sweet cherries
1 can (13 1/3 oz) pineapple titbits
1 can (11 oz) mandarin orange segments
1 cup seedless green grapes
1 tart apple
(McIntosh, Granny Smith are good choices; refer to TIPS Section - pages 216-218 for other selections of tart apples)

SOUR CREAM-HONEY DRESSING

1/2 cup dairy sour cream
1 tbsp honey
1 tbsp orange juice

Have all fruit chilled.

Just before serving, drain canned fruit thoroughly; place in large bowl.

Cut unpeeled apple into quarters; core and cut into thin wedges; add to fruit in bowl.

Mix ingredients of dressing together. Pour dressing over fruit; toss until fruit is well coated.

Serves 7-8

APPLE COLESLAW

1 head white cabbage (about 3/4 lb)
2 tart apples (McIntosh, Granny Smith are good choices; refer to TIPS Section-pages 216-218 for other selections of tart apples)
3 tbsp lemon juice
2 carrots
1/2 cup mayonnaise
salt and pepper to taste

Finely shred the cabbage with a sharp knife, discarding the central core. Put the shredded cabbage into a large bowl.

Coarsely grate the apples without peeling them. Sprinkle 2 tbsp of the lemon juice over the grated apples to prevent browning.

Scrape the carrots, then grate coarsely. Add the apple and carrots to the cabbage and toss well.

Add the mayonnaise with the remaining lemon juice and season with salt and pepper to taste. Add to the cabbage mixture; toss thoroughly and transfer to serving dish. Serve immediately.

NOTE: This coleslaw may be made in advance if you omit the grated apple. Just before serving time, prepare the apple, toss in and serve.

VARIATION: Replace the mayonnaise with 1/2 cup sour cream and 2 tablespoons milk; this will reduce the calories as well as provide a lighter flavour.

1/2 cup coarsely shredded Cheddar or Gruyere cheese may be added for extra flavour.

APPLE AND WALNUT SALAD

(Often referred to as the "Waldorf Salad" because it was first created by the chef of the Waldorf-Astoria Hotel in New York City.)

1 lb crisp, eating apples
    (a mixture of red- and green-skinned apples makes an attractive salad)
2 tbsp lemon juice
1 tsp granulated white sugar
3/4 cup mayonnaise
1/2 head celery, chopped
1/2 cup walnuts, chopped
1 head lettuce, leaves separated (optional)

Quarter and core the apples, but do not peel them. Dice them neatly and put into a bowl. Add the lemon juice and toss well to prevent discolouration.

Stir in the sugar and 1 tbsp of the mayonnaise. Mix until the apple is well coated, then leave in a cool place until ready to serve.

Just before serving, add the remaining mayonnaise, celery and walnuts and toss well together.

Serve.

This salad is very attractive when served in a bowl lined with lettuce leaves. You may garnish with a border of thinly-sliced apples (sprinkled with lemon juice) and whole walnuts.

APPLE-CABBAGE SLAW

4 cups shredded green cabbage
(1/2 medium cabbage)
1/2 cup mayonnaise
4 1/2 tsp granulated white sugar
4 1/2 tsp fresh lemon juice
1 tbsp milk
1 tsp celery seed
3/4 tsp salt
1/8 tsp pepper
2 apples, cored and chopped
(sprinkle with some of the lemon juice to prevent darkening)

To prepare cabbage, remove tough outer leaves and discard. Cut into quarters, cut out core and cut into thin shreds with a knife or shred on a coarse grater. In large bowl blend mayonnaise with sugar, lemon juice, milk, celery seed, salt and pepper. Add cabbage and mix well. Chill several hours. Add apple just before serving.

Makes 8 servings.

LOW-CAL JELLY SALAD SUPREME

1 pkg Jello Lite
(or other low calorie jelly dessert mix)
1/3 cup cottage cheese (1%)
1 tbsp mayonnaise (low calorie variety)
1 small apple, cored and grated
3 chopped cherries (optional)

Prepare Jello according to directions and chill till not quite set. Whip mayonnaise into Jello. Fold in the remaining ingredients. Chill until set.

VARIATION:

Change the flavour of the Jello.

Substitute the apple with 3/4 cup crushed pineapple.

APPLES STUFFED WITH CHICKEN SALAD

Combine:

1 can flaked chicken (6.5 oz)
1/2 cup chopped celery
1/4 cup sunflower seeds
1/4 cup mayonnaise
1/4 cup sour cream
1/2 tsp salt

Mix together all ingredients except apples.

Core 6 medium apples; cut top quarter off (or for decorative edges, use a zig-zag motion to make notches). Carefully remove centres from apples, leaving a 1/8" thick shell. Brush cut edges of apple shells with vinegar to prevent browning.

Chop removed apple centres and top quarters; add to chicken mixture.

Spoon chicken mixture into apple shells. Serve on lettuce leaf, if desired.

Makes 6 servings.

SECTION P

TIPS AND HELPFUL INFORMATION

APPLE MEASURES

1 lb.	= 3 medium apples
1 bushel apples	= 45-48 lbs.
	= approx. 150 apples
1 medium apple	= approx. 1 cup diced

6 med. apples (6 cups chopped) will make an 8" pie

2 cups canned apple pie filling will make an 8" pie (because the apples are already cooked)

1 apple will make approx. 4 or 5 apple rings

DRY MEASURES

1 tbsp	= 1/2 oz.	= 15 g
2 tbsps	= 1 oz.	= 25 g
4 tbsps	= 1/4 cup	= 50 g
8 tbsps	= 1/2 cup	= 100 g
16 tbsps	= 1 cup (1/2lb)	= 225 g
2 cups	= 1 lb	= 450 g
2 1/4 cups	= 1 1/2 lb	= 1/2 kg

Continued...

LIQUID MEASURES

1 tbsp	= 1/2 oz.	= 15 ml
2 tbsps	= 1 fl. oz.	= 25 ml
4 tbsps	= 1/4 cup	= 50 ml
8 tbsps	= 1/2 cup	= 100 ml
16 tbsps	= 1 cup (8 oz)	= 225 ml
16 fl.oz.	= 2 cups (1 pint)	= 450 ml
20 fl.oz.	= 21/2 cups	= 600 ml
32 fl.oz.	= 4 cups (1 quart)	= 1 litre
4 quarts	= 16 cups (1 gal)	= 33/4 litres)
8 quarts	= 1 peck	
4 peck	= 1 bushel	
32 quarts	= 1 bushel	

SPRINGFORM PAN:

is one where the sides can be detached from the bottom by releasing a catch or spring.

EMERGENCY SUBSTITUTIONS

1 cup whole milk:

Use 1/2 cup evaporated milk plus 1/2 cup cold water or 1/2 cup skim milk powder plus 1 cup water plus 21/2 tsp butter or margarine

1 cup sour milk or buttermilk:

Use 1 tbsp lemon juice or vinegar plus enough milk to make 1 cup; let stand for 5 minutes

1/2 cup sour cream:

Use 1/2 cup yogurt plus 1/2 tsp cornstarch

1 cup tomato juice:

Use 1/2 cup tomato catsup plus 1/2 cup water

1 Square (1 ounce) unsweetened chocolate:

Use 3 tbsp dry cocoa plus 1 tbsp butter or margarine

1 cake compressed yeast:

Use 1 package or 2 teaspoons active dry yeast

1 tbsp cornstarch:

Use 2 tbsps flour plus 4 teaspoons quick-cooking tapioca

1/2 cup dry bread crumbs (for coating food):

Use 1/2 cup well-crushed corn flakes

1/2 cup chopped nuts (for dessert toping):

Use 1/2 cup toasted rolled oats

THE VARIETIES OF APPLES

Cortland apples are large, mostly dark red apples with distinctive red stripes showing on lighter skin areas. Cortlands are all-purpose apples with fine white flesh and mild, tender taste. They are ideal for snacks, salads, and fruit plates because they stay white when cut. They make wonderful baking apples.

Crispin apples are good for pies and make a tasty fresh snack.

The **Golden Delicious** doubles as an eating and a cooking apple. A medium to large golden-yellow apple, elongated, narrowing to five-point base. Golden Delicious apples can be used for any purpose. They have white or yellowish-white, crisp flesh and very sweet taste.

Red Delicious, with its distinctive bottom bumps, is a superb eating apple. A medium to large bright red apple, sometimes showing a striped appearance. It's crisp, and sweet and is great eaten out of hand, but is not recommended for cooking.

Empire apples are medium size red apples with distinctive striped appearance. Empires are good raw but best eaten fresh from the orchard. They bake well in pies and sauces and are good for applesauce. The sweet flesh is creamy white and semi-firm.

Greening apples are large, irregular shaped, bright green (turning yellow) apples that are especially good baked.

Granny Smith apples are medium to large green apples with crisp and crunchy texture. Granny Smiths are all-purpose apples with a tart taste.

Jerseymac is a McIntosh type of apple that ripens a month earlier than McIntosh. The fruit is of good size, uniform in shape, attractive in appearance and fair to good in quality. While the trees are vigorous and productive, the fruit has a short storage life. The fruit is medium to large in size and is red with green slashes. Good for eating fresh; not especially good for baking.

Jonathan apples are medium to small sized apples with bright red colour. Jonathans are crisp, with tart flavour and are good to use raw or in pies and sauces.

Lobo apples are tart and make a refreshing snack at any time.

The **McIntosh** was developed in Ontario over 170 years ago and is harvested at the end of September or the first week of October. Medium-large apples with white flesh sometimes veined with red. Skin colour may be greenish, deeply blushed with bright red. McIntosh apples are tender and bruise easily; they are slightly tart to the taste. They're good to eat out of hand or prepared in pies and sauces. They store well for 2-3 months in regular cold storage.

Newtown Pippin are medium to very large greenish-yellow apples, sometimes blushed with pink. Crisp flesh is slightly tart. It's an excellent cooking apple.

Northern Spys and **Idareds** turn up in the best pies and are a terrific choice for any baked apple dessert. Their firm texture and rather tart flavour make them excellent cookers. Many people feel their sharp flavour makes them fine eating apples too. Northern Spys keep well for winter use.

Rome Beauty are medium-large yellow or greenish apples, usually mottled with bright red. Firm flesh is slightly tart. They are good all-purpose apples.

The **Russet** apple is a good crisp apple, sweet and tangy when eaten fresh but especially fine when baked.

Spartan apples are medium to large globular apples with bright red skins with white pin dots. They make a tasty sweet snack and an excellent, smooth pie filling.

Stayman apples are medium to large red apples. Flesh is sometimes tinged with yellow and is semi-firm in texture. Staymans have a sprightly, tart flavour and are good eaten raw or cooked in pies and sauces.

The **Winesap** apple is small to medium in size with bright red skin sometimes splotched with darker red over a distinctly yellow background. Winesap flesh is tinged with yellow and may show veins of red colour. These all-purpose apples are firm and slightly tart.

York Imperial apples are medium to large apples of solid red or pinkish red colour, often russeted. Yellowish flesh is tart and firm. York Imperials are good cooking apples.

HANDLING/SELECTING APPLES

Whichever apple variety you choose, look for fresh-looking fruit. Apples should show good colour and feel firm. Skins should be smooth and free from bruises. If you buy apples which have been pre-packed in plastic bags, inspect them to ensure good quality.

Handle apples carefully to prevent bruises.

The amounts of pectin and acid in apples vary with the variety and maturity. Crabapples, under-ripe and sour apples are high in pectin and acid. Ripe, sweet apples are high in pectin but low in acid. **When making jelly**, choose a combination of ripe and under-ripe apples. This will give the best gel as well as a better flavour.

STORING APPLES

Store apples in a either uncovered or in a perforated plastic bag in the refrigerator. If you have a large number of apples to store, keep them in a cool, dark, well-ventilated place. Warm temperatures cause apples to rapidly lose crispness and flavour, so make sure you keep them cool.

Unripe or hard apples are best held at room temperature until ready to eat. Use ripe apples within a month.

Some varieties can be stored up to two months when stored at temperatures near 0°C or 32°F with high humidity (85% or higher).

BAKING TIPS

Apples will shrink when baked. If you don't want your deep-dish pie to collapse in the centre, an inverted egg cup will hold up the pastry.

Tart apples will lose their shape when cooked so do not use them in a recipe where appearance is important.

When using raisins in a recipe, soak them in hot water for 10-15 minutes to make them plump and juicy. Drain well.

Apples will turn brown when exposed to air. This is a natural oxidation process which does not affect the taste - only the appearance - of the apple.

To prevent browning you can soak apples in a solution of:

> 2 tbsp lemon juice mixed with 1/2 cup water <u>OR</u>
>
> a solution of 1 gallon of water mixed with 2 tbsp vinegar and 2 tbsp salt.

Prevent Desserts from Sticking:

To have your cakes and desserts come out of pans without difficulty, you must "grease" your pan. To "grease", you may:

- spray with a purchased "no-stick" product
- use lard or shortening and rub (using waxed paper or fingers) all over the inside of pan
- use lard or shortening and rub (using waxed paper or fingers) all over the inside of pan then put 2 tbsp all-purpose flour in pan. Shake flour around in pan until pan is thoroughly coated.
- use lard or shortening and rub (using waxed paper or fingers) all over the inside of pan. Line bottom of pan with a piece of waxed paper cut to fit.

DID YOU KNOW?

Apples are excellent diuretics (help prevent retention of fluids).

A medium apple contains about 70 calories. It adds bulk to the diet to aid digestion, and supplies vitamins, as well as potassium and other minerals.

Spices are best if fresh. Your cinnamon begins to loose its flavour after 6 months. Store in a cool, dark, dry place.

SERVING IDEAS

Serve raw crisp apple slices and cheddar cheese for a light, delightful dessert.

Spread peanut butter on apple slices for a snack the kids will love.

Add chopped apples to poultry or pork stuffing for great flavour.

Cole slaw and tuna salad will taste even better when you add chopped apples.

A baked apple makes a great dessert, but try it for breakfast, too.

For a super side dish, saute apples and onions in bacon fat and serve with a sprinkle of grated Parmesan cheese.

Serve a surprise - stuff baked apples. Before baking, slice off the top and scoop out apple core and some of the flesh. Fill with crumbled sausage mixed with extra apple and bake until tender.

In recipe planning, count on three medium apples per pound. One pound of unpeeled apples yields about three cups of peeled, sliced or diced fruit.

Use an apple as a candle holder. Core apple; adjust size of hole to fit candle; add a tartan bow, a cinnamon stick decoration and you're set!